toddlers are a✳︎✳︎holes

{It's Not Your Fault}

By Bunmi Laditan

WORKMAN PUBLISHING • NEW YORK

A version of this book was previously self-published by the author.

Library of Congress Cataloging-in-Publication Data is available.

ISBN 978-0-7611-8564-2

DESIGN BY Nick Caruso
ILLUSTRATIONS BY Tim Tomkinson

Workman books are available at special discounts when purchased in bulk for premiums and sales promotions as well as for fund-raising or educational use. Special editions or book excerpts also can be created to specification. For details, contact the Special Sales Director at the address below, or send an email to specialmarkets@workman.com.

WORKMAN PUBLISHING COMPANY, INC.
225 Varick Street
New York, NY 10014-4381
workman.com

Printed in the United States of America

First printing March 2015

10 9

This book is dedicated to my adorable assholes. Despite making my hair fall out, I think we have a good thing going.

Contents

Dear Reader,

Whether you're reading this by the light of your phone while locked in the closet or in the car as your toddler snores behind you: Welcome.

There's a reason toddlers are at peak cuteness. It's because Nature knows that toddlerhood is when you are most likely to take your child to a public park and leave him there with a note that says, "I'm a little shit and they couldn't take it anymore."

"Toddler assholery" is a normal part of human development. It's like puberty but focuses mainly on throwing food on the floor and taking swings at people who pay your way.

Toddlers are assholes. They just are. Remind yourself of this the next time your two-year-old tosses a full bowl of oatmeal across the room. The oatmeal he cried for. The oatmeal you dragged your sleep-deprived ass out of bed at 4:45 a.m. to make.

Remind yourself of this when you're about to judge your stay-at-home spouse for the mess in the living room. He's been under house arrest with a little asshole all day.

When you feel tempted to ask your friend with a three-year-old why she doesn't call you or hang out anymore, remember that she's being held hostage. Offer to babysit while she roams Target for several hours, eating popcorn and sipping a Frappuccino.

I hope you enjoy this book. Go fill up your wineglass. You deserve it.

xo Bunmi Laditan
(aka Sopha King Tyerd)

P.S. Who is Sopha King Tyerd? Sopha King Tyerd is the parent who usually comes out between 10:00 p.m. and 5:00 a.m. She's not interested in impressing other parents or putting on airs. She might walk around for hours with a sticker on her ass and her shirt inside out. She's definitely the mom who forgets it's picture day and shows up to school drop-off looking like an extra from *Les Misérables*.

She loves her kids and is just trying to get through the hard times without losing her mind. She's too exhausted to be anything but blunt. She's Sopha King Tyerd. So fucking tired. She's who I became when I stopped pretending that I had it all under control and realized that raising kids isn't about perfection, holiday cards, or Pinterest meals. It's about experiencing the ups and the downs with the people who mean the most to you in the world.

I'm definitely Sopha King Tyerd and bet that you are, too.

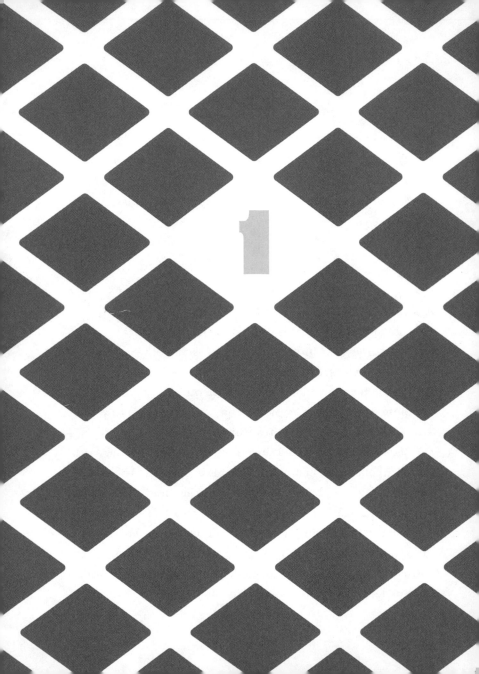

1

What Is a Toddler? And Other Frequently Asked Questions

What Is a Toddler?

A toddler is a cross between a sociopath, a rabid animal, a cocker spaniel, a demon, and an angel. Depending on the time of day and when your toddler's last meal was, you will see all of these sides.

The Average Toddler's Schedule:

3:00 A.M. Wake up with a cry so loud that it sends a rush of adrenaline through your parent's body, causing significant and permanent damage to her central nervous system.

3:01 A.M. Demand breakfast at decibel levels more suitable for raves and political protests.

3:02 A.M. Laugh in your parent's face as she tries to get you back to sleep.

3:03 A.M. Eat a NutriGrain bar on the living room floor while your parent sits slumped over on the couch trying not to cry.

3:04 A.M. Spiral kick your way through a diaper change.

3:05 A.M. Wail for no reason and demand television.

3:07 A.M. Crumble NutriGrain bar in your hand and smash it into your hair with a crazy look in your eyes.

3:15 A.M. Watch cartoons with the sleeve of Ritz crackers your parent threw at you in desperation.

4:00 A.M. Pee on the floor.

4:15 A.M. Briefly fall asleep.

4:45 A.M. Wake up angry about falling asleep.

5:00 A.M. Cry in your parent's ear while jumping on her breasts.

7:00 A.M. Snack time. Eat almost none of it.

8:00 A.M. Nap because, yes, you woke up that fucking early.

9:00 A.M. More TV because your parent can't deal with you.

10:00 A.M. TO 5:00 P.M. Destroy the house or day care. Make it look like a FEMA-neglected natural disaster area. Nap sporadically.

5:00 P.M. Get thrown at whichever parent is having the most manageable panic attack.

6:00 P.M. Ruin dinner for everyone.

7:00 P.M. Go batshit crazy about bath/brushing teeth/pajamas. It's important to act like this is your first time going through the bedtime routine.

9:00 P.M. Pass out.

To a sanctiparent (see box on next page), this will look insane. Regular parents of toddlers recognize this as their life.

THE SANCTIPARENT

Note to Sanctiparents: Shut the fuck up. Nobody wants to hear your strategies for dealing with your perfect children who wear $300 European designer tunics and shit rainbows and gold coins. When we want to hear your amazing disciplinary techniques, we'll ask. Go ahead and keep Instagramming your family's meals of figs, brown rice, breast-milk lentil soup, and homemade goat cheese from your free-range backyard talking goats. But if you humblebrag one more time about how your toddler has been sleeping through the night since he was four minutes old, we're going to pull that stick out of your ass and beat you with it. *P.S.* Keep pretending on Facebook that you're a perfect parent, but, remember, some of us know you in real life.

What Do Toddlers Want?

Your soul. Just kidding. Toddlers want whatever pops into their heads at any given moment. The problem is, these thoughts don't stop. This is why even though your toddler specifically asked for crackers, in the time it takes you to walk to the kitchen, pull the crackers out of the pantry, put the crackers on a plate, and walk back to your toddler, he now wants a piece of toast in the shape of Jay Leno's chin. Did I mention that he is also heartbroken and furious that you have presented him with disgusting offensive crackers that have no meaning to him? These crackers are no longer just crackers. They represent his frustration with having a parent who can't meet his needs. Your child might feel the need to remove all of his clothing and cry on the floor for twenty minutes, ultimately pissing himself, even though you're late for work. WELCOME TO TODDLERHOOD.

Toddlers Want to Move

Have you ever looked at a two-year-old running around and thought, "Are you on cocaine?" The reason why you're exhausted at the end of each and every day is because toddlers' bodies are constantly in motion. You literally spend your entire day trying to keep them from breaking their faces on the floor as they run at the speed of light. Being a toddler is a never-ending episode of *American Ninja Warrior,* and the only prize is a visit to the emergency room.

Toddlers Want Snacks

All this running around like they're on dirty meth can really work up an appetite. Sixty to eighty percent of caring for toddlers is simply fetching them snacks as if you were some kind of unpaid waiter. Toddlers like to eat. And by eat, I mean graze and demand food. What kind of food? Toddlers like new, exciting snacks all the fucking time, which will drive you insane by 10:00 a.m. Some toddlers may take a bite or two of the meal you've made so lovingly, but most will not finish it. You'll then feel compelled to eat the rest of their fish sticks or cheese cubes. Try not to dwell on the fact that you're eating trash. Don't worry, these calories don't count. Most of you will spend your days eating your toddler's scraps like some kind of Lululemon-wearing vulture.

The next time the Internet pressures you to shape your kid's spaghetti and meatballs into a Pixar scene like some kind of over-achiever, just say no. She's not going to eat that shit anyway. If you have a toddler who eats well, shut up about it and keep that information to yourself.

Why Is Having a Toddler So Hard?

Because they can't be reasoned with. See, adults are used to dealing with people who can work out their issues by talking, or at least posting a passive-aggressive Facebook status.

This is how an average conversation goes with a toddler:

DAD: *"Hey, buddy, we need to get dressed so that we can leave for the park."*

TODDLER: *"I want to go to the park."*

DAD: *"I know. So let's get dressed."*

TODDLER: *"No, I no want get dressed go to park now."*

DAD: *"But you're naked. You can't be naked at the park."*

TODDLER: (Crying and screaming, maybe pissing the floor, at the same time splashing urine on father, accidentally kicking dad in the nuts): *"NO GET DRESSED PARK! NO SHOES PARK! NO PANT!"*

At this point the dad is wishing he'd masturbated in the shower instead of conceiving this crazy mofo.

Toddlers look like babies, but don't get it twisted—babies are pretty easy to dress. Babies don't try to hit you. Babies don't lower your self-esteem by commenting on how big your ass looks and asking if you have to buy clothes at a special store for said large ass.

Toddlers walk through life like we all wish we could: confident, demanding, and 100 percent positive that they are the center of the universe. They can kick their father in the testicles and feel nothing. They love to laugh. They love to destroy expensive cosmetics and to fingerpaint with long-wearing lipstick. Toddlers love to render electronic devices useless. They enjoy making debit cards and keys vanish into thin air. They like to permanent marker on shit.

Toddlers live that #thuglyfe better than any of us could even try to because toddlers. don't. give. a. fuck. The quicker you understand that, the better. Repeat after me: Toddlers don't care and they never did.

Does My Toddler Hate Me?

Like serial killers, toddlers struggle with empathy. When your toddler wakes you up with a kick to the head, realize it's not because she hates you, but because she views you as a slave. You see, toddlers are primarily concerned with meeting their own needs and do not recognize that you, too, are a human person. To a toddler, you do not have a heart, mind, or soul; you are simply a skin-covered robot tall enough to reach the candy on top of the fridge. You are an epidermis bag and source of endless comfort. Don't take your toddler's antics personally, because it isn't about you.

THE SANCTIPARENT

"Children are a blessing from above, and you do not deserve kids if you don't feel this way. I feel sorry for your toddler."

RESPONSE: "I know my toddler is a blessing. I'm reminded of this every April. Tax Deduction."

Why Don't Toddlers Listen?

Contrary to popular opinion, toddlers do not possess listening ears. They are unable to hear commands like "Stop," "No," "Don't eat your boogers," or "Stop lifting mommy's skirt." Toddlers can only hear words that pertain to snacks. A toddler may not understand the words "Stay in your bed," but she will hear you chewing a Mentos from outer space.

Toddlers live by one simple rule: DO THE OPPOSITE.

If you tell a toddler to wave to a shop owner, she will stand there like she can't speak. If you tell a toddler to say hello to a family member, he will stand there like a Precious Moments figurine. If you tell a toddler to keep breathing, she will hold her breath until she passes out. Toddlers live to disobey. Once you understand this, you can control them through reverse psychology—in layman's terms, *mind-fucking*.

How Do I Deal with My Toddler's Behavior?

Do what most parents do and drown your frustrations in dough-nuts and beer come bedtime. Personal trainers and fitness nuts will tell you that eating before bed is bad for your health and waistline. What these idiots don't understand is that you need to snack so that you don't abandon your family in the night.

When it comes down to it, isn't it preferable to inhale a bag of Doritos and be forty or fifty pounds overweight than to leave your toddler without a parent? You're doing the right thing by eating your emotions. Living with a toddler isn't the time for you to be worried about having a thigh gap. Fun fact: You can actually create a thigh gap no matter what you weigh just by standing with your legs apart. See? Gap. (But, remember, thigh gaps are dangerous because toddlers can use them to climb back into your uterus.)

It's possible that you can get so depressed from living with a toddler that you may need prescription medication from an actual doctor. I'm telling you, having a toddler is no fucking joke. In that case, be sure to jot down whatever antidepressants you're taking and the dosage in your child's baby book. When she looks back on her milestones, she'll also see the damage she did to your mental health. Hopefully, this will inspire her to major in something serious like biology or political science rather than ceramics, so she'll be able to take care of you the way you

(*continued on page 14*)

R_X

PATIENT: _____   DATE: _____

ADDRESS: _____

_____

PHONE: _____

❏ REFILL   ❏ DO NOT REFILL

LATE NIGHT FOOD PRESCRIPTION:
(Take this to any convenience store.)

MEDICINE:

Chocolate • Bagels and cream cheese • Fruit cup
(Just kidding, this one is a joke. Fruit can't solve
problems.) • Bags of Skittles • Twix bars • Reese's
Peanut Butter Cups • Snickers bars • Unlimited
popcorn • Cookies • Expired Halloween candy
(They keep this in the back.) • Ice cream • Frozen
appetizers like potato skins with Cheddar cheese
and bacon • Wine • Rum • Any other liquor
• Healthy vegetable juice (for your kids) • Beer

RECIPES
for Parents on the Edge

No one is going to judge you for shame-eating Peeps in December to get through potty training. Everybody does it. Get fancy and try out some crazy recipes. Ideas below.

"SWEET AS LIFE USED TO BE" DESSERT NACHOS

Layer Cinnamon Toast Crunch, melted butter, and crushed-up Pop-Tarts. Put in oven on 300°F to warm. Eat standing up over garbage can.

"WHY DON'T-U-LISTEN?" TRAIL MIX

Take revenge on your small child by mixing all his favorite snacks in a large bowl. Throw in Goldfish crackers, Gummy vitamins, yogurt-covered raisins, cereal, and whatever else you can find. Eat by the greedy-ass handful while you watch people succeed on TV.

HOPELESSNESS DIP

In a semiclean Tupperware container, melt one cup of shredded cheese and a half cup of Velveeta. Mix in some sour cream to taste and a packet of French onion dip. Eat with tortilla chips until you can't feel anything.

ANGER GUMBO

Melt three cups of ice cream in a large bowl. Add brownie pieces, M&Ms, marshmallows, and Golden Grahams cereal. Drizzle with three shots of low-grade tequila. Garnish with whipped topping. Slurp up with a spoon until you're a little less afraid of morning.

FRUSTRATION SALAD

In a medium bowl, mix together crumbled bacon, chopped hard-boiled eggs, and lots of mayonnaise. Eat at 2:00 a.m. while crying.

GREEN SMOOTHIES

Blend up vodka and mint chip ice cream. *Bam.* There's calcium in there, too. Calcium for your bones. Add whipped cream for additional vitamin D.

vodka   +   *mint chip ice cream*   +   *blender*

(continued from page 10)

deserve. No one ever made millions handcrafting clay pots. It's her turn to foot the bill.

Parents, there is no shame in being medicated. Like I said, at least you're still there. Anything you can do to keep from packing up your shit and leaving is called love.

Are Toddlers Crazy?

Precisely. Toddlers are nuts and will make you crazy, too. If you have a toddler in your home, it's best to imagine that you live in a circus with an emotionally unstable ringleader. This way, when he throws a shoe at your head and rage-vomits, you can shake your head and know that it has nothing to do with you and every-thing to do with him.

Toddlers can go from laughing to crying to screaming in a matter of seconds. There is no point in trying to keep up with their tsunami of emotions, because as you're addressing one, the next one is already revving up to drown you. When you get over-whelmed by your toddler's feelings, it's best just to find a quiet corner where you can hug your knees and rock back and forth. Sing a pretty, sad song like "The Rose." You can even make up your own tune. My favorite is "I Used to Have Dreams." After a few minutes your kid will seek you out, sit on your head, and fart, but at least you tried. This is called yoga.

How Do I Become a Better Parent?

Who cares? Right now your job as a parent is to survive. You are in the trenches with a psychopath. Remember that. This isn't the time to play Holier Than Thou Parent. It's time to make it to the next day.

How Do I Know If I Have a Toddler?

You know you have a toddler if . . .

1. You hate your spouse a little. Toddlers can destroy your marriage if you let them. The stress of living in an insane asylum with a child who makes you want to fall on your sword will take a toll on your personal relationship. People without a toddler of their own will not understand how someone so cute will make you want to be single, living in a studio apartment with only a bottle of Jose Cuervo to keep you company. You don't actually hate your spouse, it just feels like it because you hate life. Do not let your little cockblock tear your love life apart. Remember: You're in a war zone. You need backup.

2. You no longer fantasize about being rich, famous, beautiful, or talented. Your fantasies now center around sleep. You dream about being rested and floating away on a California king bed where you can lie in starfish formation. Toddlers have the potential to steal just as many Z's as their infant brethren. Infants don't scream in your face. Infants don't run into traffic. It's a hard truth to swallow, but with a toddler you will be more physically and emotionally tired than you have ever been while also having to deal with twilight shenanigans that will astonish you nightly.

3. You have become a shut-in. Hopefully you have a backyard, because you're going to lose your will to leave the house. It just won't be worth it anymore. Why deal with dressing a toddler, car-seat drama, and a public meltdown when you can just become a recluse? Groceries are available for purchase online. Get some vitamin D capsules to make up for the sunlight you won't be getting anymore.

4. You've hauled a kid out of a grocery store under your arm like a bundle of firewood in front of a crowd of gawking strangers. Good for you. Angry whispering can only get you so far. Abandon that cart of groceries. Don't abandon the wine, though. That's crazy. Pay for the wine. Throw $20 at the cashier and tell her to keep the change.

5. You regularly open packages of food in stores to keep your baboon quiet while you shop. Don't worry; it's not shoplifting until you forget to pay.

6. You've had to alert a store employee to the fact that your kid has urinated on their floor. Hey, better a linoleum floor than a stack of neatly folded sweaters. Bonus points if your toddler has ever thrown up in public. On you. When you don't have a change of clothes.

7. You sometimes wish you had a time machine and a condom.

8. You have stress-induced heart palpitations. No, your child is not trying to kill you, but she might by accident.

9. You've seriously considered starting a new life in a new city. If you do this, be sure to cut up your credit cards. They can be used to track you.

10. You have more gates up in your home than the local zoo.

11. You know that "My phone is charging" is code for "I need you to lay off my shit and play with your own toys."

12. Your sex life has come to a standstill. Toddlers are natural birth control. Their antics will cause your sex organs to shrivel into your body and seal off. (See Chapter 14.)

13. You've seriously researched sleep-away preschools.

14. Every one of your cabinets has some kind of lock on it.

15. Bedtime in your house looks like spring break in Cancún.

16. All four food groups can be found between your couch cushions.

17. You've had to say "Stop eating out of the trash" in the last twenty-four hours.

18. A small child has recently blown his nose into your shirt.

19. You would give your molars for a free, reliable babysitter. Who needs to chew meat when you can go out for drinks whenever you want?

20. You wonder if it would be creepy to ask teens on the street if they babysit.

21. You've fallen asleep with your eyes open.

22. You'd rather have a public colonoscopy than take your child into a store where glass items are displayed in the open.

23. You'd rather get a Pap smear from Edward Scissorhands than take your kid to a restaurant.

The Theory of Toddler Evolution

The Terrible Twos

Sure, terrible. If you say so. This is as cute as your kid is ever going to get. A two-year-old is trapped between babyhood and kidhood, and it's a beautiful thing to behold. Is there anything cuter than a two-year-old Tweedledee stumbling around?

Depending on your personal destiny, your 2T might be a sweetheart or a raving lunatic. Whatever she is, please know that her behavior will go downhill from here. Two-year-olds might not be in full toddler mode yet, but they will often show glimpses of what lies ahead.

You may notice your two-year-old, who was sleeping fantastically up until now, start to resist going to bed. He might also start waking up in the middle of the night or at 4:00 a.m. ready to start the day. This is a warning.

You've been thinking that you're a pretty amazing parent? That maybe you lucked out? Hahaha. Wait. Just wait. Even the calmest of two-year-olds is watching and learning. He is studying you to find out what your buttons are and how best to get inside your head.

If you have a two-year-old who is already batshit crazy and exhibiting many signs of assholery, at least the suspense is over. Despite the fact that your 2T can walk, she will demand to be carried everywhere. Tots don't care if you're holding $500 worth of groceries, a 300-count box of diapers, and their baby sibling—they want up and they want it now. Prepare to spend hours of your life watching your toddler sit on the ground pretending her legs stopped working, *Secret Garden*-style. Wait her out. You only have one back, and if you waste it lugging around a kid who can walk, by the time you hit empty nest you'll be immobile. Spend big bucks on toddler carriers if you'd like, but know that your money could also be going toward margarita mix.

Two-year-olds are next to impossible to understand, and they feel self-conscious about how much they suck at speaking. This is why asking a 2T to repeat himself sends him into a rage. Pretend to understand his gibberish or you'll get bitch-slapped. Two-year-olds are cute, but never, ever mistake their elfin good looks for kindness.

A two-year-old's spirit animal is a puppy—puppies are playful, they shit everywhere, and they're more work than you thought. Their adorableness makes it all worthwhile, but at the same time, you're getting tired of cleaning up poop. They make messes bigger than you could ever have imagined and require enormous amounts of supervision and attention.

One thing to be aware of is how surprisingly strong two-year-olds are. Do NOT become one of the many parents who have received a black eye from their young toddler. Ask a group of dads and you'll find one whose toddler has blown out one of his testicles. Literally blown it out. Popped it through force so that it's rendered useless like an empty water balloon.

Two-year-olds' heads are reinforced with steel. If that dome connects to your own head or eye, you will black out. There's no use getting mad. Next time, stay alert.

The Thankless Threes

Age three is when your toddler enters full asshole mode. Three-year-olds spend most of their awake time crying, crying louder, and then scream-crying. When they're not doing that, they're whining and making a scene. Three-year-olds have only one goal: to make you look like a bitch-ass punk in public. Once you know this, you'll pick your battles. Pick none of them. Don't engage in arguments with a three-year-old, because if you're yelling or explaining, they've already won. Three-year-olds are power-hungry despots who take pleasure in seeing you become unhinged. Keep a flask close at hand and take a hit whenever you feel your blood pressure rising.

It's important to know that three-year-olds believe that they are victims. They also believe that they are royalty. They believe that everything they want, whether it is a new My Little Pony Rainbow Dash or a grilled cheese sandwich with no crust, cheese, or bread, should be delivered immediately on a golden platter.

When you disappoint a three-year-old, he descends into an uncontrollable rage, and his anger knows no bounds. A 3T will cut you where it hurts. His impressive vocabulary will string together all sorts of insults. Age three is when you will most likely wonder if you have given birth to the anti-Christ. If a three-year-old could cut off your finger with a *katana* as a punishment for putting her toast on the wrong plate, she would. Not because she hates you, but because she is an emotionally unstable being who does not live beyond the present moment. Three-year-olds don't just carpe the diem, they carpe your will to take them anywhere. They do best in groups with other three-year-olds. In a community of their peers, these toddlers will create complicated *Lord of the Flies* hierarchies rich with unspoken rules and contracts. Don't try to make sense of it, just enjoy that they're not giving you hell for five minutes.

Three-year-olds cry more often than newborn babies. The level of drama they bring into a home (especially if they are a middle child) will drain you daily. On the plus side, kids in this age group are highly intelligent. They also tend to behave well when not in the presence of their parental units.

A three-year-old's spirit animal is the wolverine. Wolverines hail from the weasel family and are thought to have somewhat demonic ferocity that is disproportionate to their size. They are fearless hunters and have been known to take down bears. Their encounters with humans are devastating (but you already know this, don't you?). They are known to be extremely territorial. Have you ever seen the way a three-year-old looks at his new baby sibling? You'll notice that he seems eerily calm, his eyes dead as he waits for an opportunity to do something bad.

Note: Avoid eye contact with three-year-olds when they are hungry or tired. Like violent dogs, they assume you are challenging them and will charge. Too many people have lost nipples and eyelids to the teeth of three-year-olds. Too many.

The Fucking Fours

Right now you're wondering if a four-year-old is a toddler. The answer is: Kinda. Age four is the last year of the toddler stage, right at the edge of big-kidness. Four-year-olds believe that they are rock stars. Divas. Celebrities. The good news is that they've burned off most of the poison gas that drives three-year-olds' behavior. The bad news is that they operate on the assumption that if you don't bow down to them, it's because you're jealous. Four-year-olds are a cross between Charlie Sheen, Lindsay Lohan, and Stephen Hawking: They don't seem to learn from their mistakes, are highly unpredictable, but show sparks of pure genius.

Four-year-olds love to argue and will surprise you by calling you out on your lies and inconsistencies. This is irritating. Four-year-olds are like three-year-olds but better at pressing your buttons. Keep in mind that when your four-year-old is upset, she can make quite a scene. Being older means that her lungs are more developed and her screams carry farther. But now that you know what matters to her, it will be easier to customize threats to control her behavior.

Bribes work much better with four-year-olds than with younger toddlers because they now understand the purpose of money.

Try to get your four-year-old into some kind of preschool or military academy. Four-year-olds are surprisingly good at following instructions when given by people who don't love them. If you're at home with a four-year-old all day, try to go outside. Nature will help you coparent. Nature will share custody of your child. Indoors, four-year-olds are known to be clingy and will constantly be trying to reenter the womb or, if you're male, trying to meld their skin to yours.

Four-year-olds can be fun to take places, as most of them are fully potty trained. This isn't to say that they can't have accidents, so ask them every five minutes if they need to use the bathroom. Remember: The first "no" is usually a lie. Ask again. Then again.

Toddler Preparedness Kit

If you're a new toddler parent, it can be helpful to make yourself a toddler preparedness kit. These aren't sold in stores, so you'll have to fashion your own. Pull together the following items:

BABY WIPES: These aren't for your kid's butt, they're for yours. Since you won't have time to shower anymore (unless you want to do it with a kid sitting at your feet, staring at your genitals and asking questions), it's good to keep a box of a wipes around to keep your nethers reasonably fresh. As always, wipe from front to back to avoid a bladder infection. You don't have time for doctor's appointments. Moms: It can be tempting to neglect your downstairs area, but if you do, you'll get enough yeast infections to start baking vagina bread.

ASPIRIN/TYLENOL: Sleep deprivation = regular headaches.

VITAMINS: Try to remember to take these. You're going to need all the help you can get. Plus, if you get sick, nobody will take care of you.

NETFLIX SUBSCRIPTION: Say good-bye to seeing movies in the theater. You will watch them on Netflix four years after the general public. You will not be able to stay awake, so it will take you approximately three months to get through the average ninety-minute movie. Because of this, you will have no fucking idea what the movie is about. Wikipedia can fill in the blanks.

TIC TACS: Buy these in bulk and always have them on hand to bribe your kid to act right in public. Tic Tacs are also a dentist-approved alternative to brushing your teeth.

STICKERS: Stickers are currency in the toddler community. Yes, they'll end up in the most annoying places (like your butt crack), but they can also prevent grocery-store meltdowns. Don't worry if your kids eat most or all of the stickers you give them. They'll reappear in three to four hours covered in feces.

SMARTPHONE WITH A GOOD DATA PLAN: The Internet is your portal to the rest of the world. The people online are your only friends.

BLANKET FOR CAR NAPS: Should your toddler fall asleep in the car on the way home NEVER attempt the mythical vehicle-to-bed transfer. Your kid will wake up partially rested and the next 24–48 hours will be hell. Pull into the driveway, put the car in park, and leave the engine on. (If you turn the engine off, your child will wake up—so fuck global warming.) Lock the doors, pull that blanket around your face, and pass out.

Grooming Your Goblin

Once you have a toddler, each day will begin and end with a tango known as "Changing Clothes," or, as many parents call it, "What the Fuck Is Wrong with You?"

Despite the fact that your toddler has to get dressed each and every day of her life, she will act surprised as hell that you want to cover her nakedness.

A key part of getting clothes onto a toddler is to use the element of surprise. Do not prepare him or he'll run. You may have to use MMA moves to keep your child still as you remove his ten-pound pee-filled nighttime diaper. Getting a shirt over his big toddler head will be difficult. Look for shirts with wide openings. (For some reason, clothing manufacturers are under the impression that toddlers have normal-size domes. This is a lie. Toddler heads make up three fourths of their body weight.)

Do your best to snake those flailing limbs through the T-shirt holes. By now your toddler is screaming and may have tried to hit you. Your neighbors may be dialing 911, so if you hear cops at the door, answer promptly. Do whatever it takes to get pants on your lunatic. Socks will be difficult to put on her windmilling legs, but try. Don't bother with shoes unless you have plans to leave immediately. If you put them on beforehand, they will be removed and lost in the house for good. You will never find those things again until you sell your house and are packing up to move. Actually, you will find one, which is worse.

Once your toddler is dressed, shadow him to make sure he doesn't strip off his clothes. Toddlers love to ruin a finished project as a way of flipping you off.

The Rat's Nest

Toddler hair isn't worth dealing with. If you have a boy, just try to keep it short. Use craft scissors while he's sleeping and aim for a respectable shape. If you have a girl, follow the same instructions. Toddlers hate getting their hair brushed and will howl like wolves if you attempt it. If you have somewhere important to go, like a funeral or a modeling casting appointment, just spray your kid's hair with water. Wet hair usually looks better.

The Fangs

Brush your toddler's teeth if you have energy for it at the end of the day. Who gives a fuck. If their teeth rot out of their head, you can sleep easy knowing that a second set of grownup teeth are on their way. Baby teeth are like condoms—they're meant to be thrown away after use. Keep them clean if you can, but don't stress yourself. If your family dentist tries to make you feel bad about your toddler's cavities, just say, "My failure is paying your bills, so shut it." Anyway, the #1 use of toddler teeth is to draw blood.

The proper way to brush a toddler's teeth:

1. Tell toddler it's time to brush teeth.

2. Chase toddler around house.

3. Pry mouth open.

4. Try to weasel toothbrush into mouth without scraping gums.

5. Apologize for scraping gums.

6. Explain that you can't put Band-Aids on mouth boo-boos.

7. Listen to toddler complain about how "spicy" the bubble gum–flavored toothpaste is.

8. Hold back tears when toddler bites your finger.

9. Tell toddler he has to open mouth more than 1 millimeter.

10. Tell toddler not to swallow toothpaste.

11. Watch toddler swallow toothpaste.

12. Tell toddler to spit in the sink.

13. Watch toddler spit on the counter.

14. Yell to spouse that you need to tap out.

The Epidermis

Toddlers eat so much butter that their skin is always perfectly moisturized. If you ever run out of butter for, say, corn on the cob, you can actually just run your warm corn down your toddler's arm and it will be nicely coated in a sweet and salty milk-based film. Go ahead. It's edible. Treat yourself!

Ironically, toddlers will also eat your lotion. Keep it on a high shelf. The odd taste will not stop your wildebeest from downing an entire bottle of Saint Ives Vanilla Apple Orchard. Toddlers don't care.

Try to clean your toddler's neck every now and then. If you don't, a black ribbon of dust and grime will accumulate Oliver Twist–style. Get behind her ears with a damp washcloth and give it a solid wipe. You may have to hold her down to do this, because toddlers like to be dirty.

Bathtime aka Waterworld

Parents love bathtime because it means that bedtime is near.

To prepare your darling for her bath, put on your full-length poncho, because toddlers don't bathe, they splash, motherfucker. When toddlers bathe, they act like they're a junior member of the summer Olympics diving team. Get ready. By the time you're done, your bathroom floor will have a few inches of standing water. The good news is that wiping up all that water counts as mopping the floor.

Buy bath toys if you want, but what toddlers really love are kitchen utensils. The weirder the utensil (couscous sieve, egg smasher), the more likely your kid will need that shit in the bath on the immediate. Give it to her. Throw in a couple of Tupperware containers, too.

The amount of crap in your tub will rival that in your garage. By the time you go to take a shower, it'll be like cleansing yourself inside a dollar store. Try not to slip—you could end up with a spoon enema. (Unless you're into that, then slip away.)

You should know that it's perfectly normal for assholes to cry about taking a bath and then cry when they have to get out. Don't try to wrap your mind around that. It is what it is. Never blame yourself for your toddler's shortcomings. You gave her life.

Note: Toddlers love bubbles. While the water is running, squirt in some dish soap. Agitate the water to keep the bubbles active. Your toddler will come out squeaky clean.

Eau de Toddler

What is a toddler supposed to smell like? Toddlers smell like farts, old milk, diarrhea, and lunch meat. That fresh newborn smell went away the minute the child started eating processed solid foods.

Toddler Clothes: A Retail Guide

Where all your money goes.

TARGET Four-dollar pants and shirts. You can dress your entire kid for a year for the price of an oil change.

ETSY This is the place to shop if you don't mind spending $140 on an ensemble. Be aware that if you make Etsy your go-to store, your child will end up looking like some kind of hobbit or Dr. Seuss character. None of this shit is machine washable, because it was hand-sewn by a raw-vegan lunatic living in Oregon who sleeps in a tree.

WALMART More cheap clothing. Always buy one size up so your child's clothes never fit correctly. It'll make you feel like a planner.

RICHER CHILDREN Do your best to befriend a parent with a child 1–2 years older than yours. Shamelessly beg for their cast-offs. If these parents don't plan on having any more kids but have expensive taste for quality clothes, you've just won the lottery. Do whatever it takes to keep these people happy. Surprise them with wine. Go on and on about how poor you are and how cold your child is every winter.

THRIFT STORES A great place to get clothes for your toddler. You can find name brands at well below retail. The only downside is that you have to riffle through a lot of crappy shit and might bring home bedbugs.

Mealtime
aka Hell

Mealtime with a toddler can only be described as a fat pain in the ass. It's best if you don't expect to eat. Don't even set a place for yourself at the table. Just stand next to your toddler like the hired help. You will spend the entire time getting up, fetching things from the kitchen, making empty threats about dessert, and blowing on food that is no longer hot.

Dinner with a Toddler: What to Expect

The first thing toddlers do when they sit down for a meal is urgently need to shit. This is universal.

When you're back from the bathroom with the scent of poo still in your nose, the next thing your toddler will do, if he is in a good mood, is begin to talk. He won't stop. He'll ramble on endlessly and ignore your attempts to direct his attention to his food. If your toddler is in a bad mood, he will cry and complain about the meal, flatware, and whatever else he can think of. Either way, no eating will be done. He'll ask you to identify every flavor, spice, and seasoning.

If your toddler does eventually eat, it will be a few bites, no more. Most toddlers eat a thimble-size amount of dinner before asking if they can have dessert.

It's best if you lie to your toddler and make him think fruit is an acceptable dessert. You and I know that fruit is never dessert, but children aren't smart enough to know different. Giving toddlers fruit for dessert is a good way to use up all the produce left over from Instagram photo shoots. Don't worry if you can't afford organic produce. If a child can lick the bottom of her own shoe and survive, chances are a regular apple isn't going to hurt her. Remember: We were raised on cans of "fruit cocktail," the kind with two bright red maraschino cherries per can. Delish!

If you opt to go the traditional route of having your child sit at a table for meals, please know that the food will end up on the floor anyway. You're wasting your time.

Vacuum up what's left at the end of the day or, like any good cell phone plan, let those minutes roll over. Cheerios are even better the next day (or week). They age like fine wine.

Why do you want your toddler to eat? Because if he doesn't eat at dinner, he'll ask for food at bedtime. The one thing you can do to make the sleep routine easier is fill up that toddler belly. Oh yeah, and nutrients are good for them or something. If your toddler refuses to eat at dinner, give him a cup of heavy cream before bed. It's worth it. Check with your pediatrician so you can't sue me if the kid gets violent diarrhea.

RECIPES
for Picky Eaters

You can go ahead and make Pinterest-worthy meals if you'd like, as long as you're okay with watching them go over the edge of a table with a child's index finger.

"IS IT BEDTIME YET?" SAVORY CHEESE CASSEROLE

You'll need two slices of white bread. Look for the unhealthiest bread you can find. You'll want it as refined as possible. It should be soft as a pillow and contain no whole grains or detectable nutrients. You can find this bread in the "I've Given Up" section of the grocery store, next to the malt liquor and rolling papers. Grab a slice of cheese. Processed cheese. This kind of cheese doesn't need to be refrigerated because it's not food.

Place the cheese product in between the two slices of bread. Melt half a cup of butter into a pan. Brown "casserole" on both sides. On a plate that your toddler is okay with (ask, don't assume), place the "Is It Bedtime Yet?" Savory Cheese Casserole and await further instructions. Your toddler will let you know with a sharp howl if he would like the crusts cut off or if he would like the casserole in a special shape.

Toddler will then take two to three mouse-size bites before asking for dessert. When you say no to dessert (because there is no fucking dessert with lunch), your toddler will cry so hard that he throws up the small amount of food he ate. Make yourself a vodka soda.

NO-EFFORT RICE PILAF

Cook some white rice. Not wild rice, not brown rice, not quinoa, WHITE RICE. Place the rice in a bowl that speaks to your toddler's mood. Serve with enough butter to clog a giant's arteries. This meal should be as shiny and yellow as the sun. Your toddler will be angry that the rice was served in a bowl, not a plate, because bowls are "for babies" today. Oh, you didn't know? Learn to read your toddler's mind. In her fury, she will knock over the bowl of rice and it will fall on the floor. Just let it sit there until it gets hard. A family of rats will gather the remnants.

ZERO-NUTRIENTS CEREAL SNACK

Pour your toddler's favorite cereal into a bowl. Add as much milk as he'd like. While he eats, pin to your "Healthy Recipes" and "Gluten-Free" Pinterest boards.

"NO COLLEGE FUND" PIZZA

Spend $40 on pizza delivery. Listen to your toddler cry for thirty minutes about how pizza is all wrong. Watch her take a small bite of crust. Google "Can anger give you a heart attack?" Start the bedtime routine.

WASTED PASTA

Make enough pasta to feed a small village. Put pasta in a bowl with some butter. Watch your toddler massage pasta into his face and hair. Ask yourself why you even bother. Give toddler a bath.

Snacktime

The best way to give a toddler a snack is to throw a handful of Cheerios on the floor and let her serve herself. Don't get your child addicted to bowls and spoons. Just throw down a sippy cup of milk in her direction and some fruit or raisins if your toddler needs additional fiber. Apple slices will keep on a carpeted or hardwood floor for up to three days in the summer and two weeks in the winter.

Couch-cushion snacks are also a great source of minerals, as they are usually coated with dust and hair. In case you didn't know, hair is made out of protein and counts as meat in a pinch. The occasional crunchy granule of gravel or sand can double as floss and remove debris from your toddler's mouth. Does your toddler eat paper? Paper comes from trees, so it's like salad. Good for you for giving your toddler vegetables! Encourage your toddler to hunt for floor food while you read *Us Weekly*. Pediatricians call this "bonding."

PUFF SNACKS: Puff snacks are sold in canisters and are always 50 percent full at the time of purchase. They cost between $50 and $100 a pop.

The only thing you need to know about the crunchy toddler snacks on the market is that you're going to end up eating 90 percent of those suckers yourself, so pick a flavor you like. They go with any drugstore liquor.

"This is terrible! No wonder kids these days are obese. My toddler loves salad and gobbles up kale from our family garden!"

RESPONSE: "Shut your damn mouth before I shut it for you."

CANDY: Is candy bad for kids? Maybe. Is being annoyed bad for parents? Definitely. Give the kids some fucking candy. If you were born before 1985, your parents fed you a steady diet of processed meats, white bread, and pickles. Remember those American cheese sandwiches? The Kool-Aid? We survived. We didn't even know what organic apples were. A lollipop isn't going to kill your kid. Not unless the top comes off and chokes her, so give that pop a good pull to make sure it's on tight.

Never give a toddler chocolate. This is inexcusable behavior. We don't waste chocolate on babies.

JUICE: It's time to calm down about juice, people. Some of you parents out there are acting like it's liquid herpes. It's juice, not blue meth. Stop saying, "My child has never had juice," like your

(continued on page 48)

Dear Asshole Whisperer,
Can my toddler live on a steady diet of white carbs and milk?
—Mom in Utah

Dear Mom in Utah,
Absolutely. Toddlers, like plants, get nutrients via photosynthesis. If your kid is on a food strike and slurping down whole milk in lieu of solids, don't get your panties/ boxer briefs in a wad. Unless your kid starts fainting, he'll probably be okay. Talk to your doctor. He might be able to get you a prescription that will make you happier.

Dear Asshole Whisperer,
I try to feed my toddler reasonably healthy food but still feel judged by other parents. What should I do?
—Mom of Two in Maine

Dear Mom of Two,
There's always going to be a parent who you feel is doing a better job than you, but think of it this way: In a zombie apocalypse, kids that smell like kefir and kombucha (i.e., rotting flesh) will get eaten first.

Dear Asshole Whisperer,
Why won't my toddler try new foods?
                    —Dad in California

Dear Dad in California,
Because it means so damn much to
you and because toddlers also have
highly sensitive taste buds. Flavors like
eggplant and whole grains make them angry,
but Cheetos seasoning is just fine. Ninety-nine percent
of your toddler's life is controlled by you. Once she
figures out that you can't actually force food down
her gullet, meal time can quickly become her main
way of expressing civil disobedience.

Dear Asshole Whisperer,
Why does it seem like my friend's kid eats better than my toddler?
                    —Mom in Wisconsin

Dear Mom in Wisconsin,
Because your friend is either: A) a fucking liar or 2) God
loves them more. Stop comparing and play the hand
you were dealt.

(continued from page 45)

kid just won a Pulitzer. Remember the generation raised on Tang and its raggedy cousin, Sunny Delight? Yeah, that was us. I'm not saying you should pump your kid full of high fructose or even the 100 percent stuff, but quit with all that sanctimonious bullshit.

Now to contradict myself: If you do bring juice into your home, know that it's the closest thing to giving your child an ecstasy pill. Your toddler will fiend for it hard. He'll pace like someone itching for a nicotine hit as you pour it, and grab it out of your hands with legit desperation. Cut it with water if you want, but have you tasted your half-juice, half-water concoctions? They taste like piss. You're the boss, though.

Dirty Ways to Trick Your Toddler into Eating

Here are five ways to get your toddler to ingest food other than milk and Ritz crackers:

1. Toddlers don't like to eat from their own plates. It's far too predictable. They much prefer raining on your own food parade by picking at your meal. When toddlers do this, it's their way of saying, "Motherfucker, I own you." If you've never tried to enjoy food while having a dirty, chubby toddler hand that has probably recently been up her butt reach onto your plate and pull off your last slice of bacon, you're living the dream. Turn this to your advantage by

loading up your plate with shit you actually want your toddler to eat and acting like you're in seventh heaven chowing down. Within moments your toddler will be at your side, begging for a piece of red pepper. Make a big show out of how you really wanted that pepper and try to force a few tears out of the corners of your eyes. The more your toddler feels like she's hurting you, the happier she'll be. If you have a particularly kind toddler, she may offer you a very small bite of your own pepper. Shake your head sadly and say, "No. It's okay. You eat it." Your toddler will feel extremely powerful.

2. Ketchup. Toddlers like ketchup because it's 99 percent sugar. Serve it on everything. There are people on Pinterest who will try to get you to make low-sugar ketchup from scratch. Tell those people you don't have time for their bullshit science projects, and give your kid the real stuff. Put it on broccoli, pizza, potatoes, cheese, whatever you want your kid to eat. I believe toddlers like it because they are soul murderers and it looks like blood.

3. Bring in an extra kid. In the same way that hyenas enjoy picking apart a fawn carcass in community, toddlers enjoy eating together. The same toddler who spends family dinners crying will spend them eating if there is just one other child present. The more kids, the better they'll eat, because it sets off the "orphanage response," which makes them worry that there won't be enough food. It's not currently possible to rent extra kids, so you'll need to make some friends. Invite them over for lunch for the sole purpose of making sure your toddler gets a week's worth of calories in a single meal. Note: This doesn't work with siblings.

4. Melted Cheese/Velveeta. Velveeta is melted cheese's broke, illegitimate step-cousin. It probably doesn't have any actual cheese but it is uniform in color and consistency and that's what matters most when you're two years old. Melted cheese can cover up all kinds of vegetables and meats. Go crazy.

5. The "one more bite" trick. Toddlers will always want to know how much food they need to pack into their bodies before you leave them alone and start the dessert course. You can use this to your advantage by repeatedly telling them they need to take "just one more bite." Because they can't count and are slow, they'll always think they're just one spoonful of casserole junk away from a brownie sundae. Keep the charade up as long as you can.

A Note About Restaurants

Do not take your toddler to a restaurant. There is no reason to do it. Even if the only things in your fridge are mayonnaise and beer, there's still Chinese food delivery (get fortune cookies for the child) or a quick run to the McDonald's drive-thru. I'd even suggest making mayonnaise and beer soup before taking your kid out to eat. The alcohol will mostly cook off.

Never, ever take your toddler to a sit-down restaurant unless it specifically caters to wild animals. If feral cats or rabid monkeys are not allowed in the restaurant, your toddler should not set foot in the establishment.

Taking a young child to a restaurant will result in a nervous breakdown for all adults involved and a reduced life expectancy of six months for every hour you spend in the eatery.

New Names for Crappy Foods

Don't feel bad if the only foods you can get into your toddler are crap. Most go through a stage where they will only eat foods that would get you kicked out of the Granola Mommies Club. Reframe that meal in your mind and, ta da! It's not as bad as you thought. Use the handy guide below.

CHICKEN NUGGETS . . . . **Authentic Breaded Chicken Morsels**

PIZZA . . . . **Rustic Italian Flatbread with Cheese Garnish**

FISH STICKS . . . . **Crispy Island Seafood Batons**

FRENCH FRIES . . . . **Hearty Potato Spears**

KETCHUP . . . . **Factory-Fresh Tomato Aioli**

FRUIT SNACKS . . . . **Dehydrated Fruit Carpaccio**

0% FRUIT JUICE . . . . **Simulated Produce Beverage**

LOLLIPOPS . . . . **Fruit on a Stick**

BUTTER . . . . **Vitamin-Fortified Hard Milk**

BEEF JERKY . . . . **Salted Protein Strips**

HERE IS WHAT WILL HAPPEN: You will walk into the restaurant full of hope. The other patrons will smile at your adorable child. You will beam with pride and think, "This time . . . this time will be different." You will be led to a dark corner in the back because the hostess knows what toddlers are like.

Then hell will begin.

Instead of leisurely browsing the menu, you will spend your time trying to get your child up from under the restaurant table. As soon as the waiter arrives with your food, your child will have to use the bathroom. There, in the porcelain confines of a public restroom, your beautiful child will take the biggest, smelliest, longest, most explosive, most repulsive shit of her life. You will be responsible for wiping said shit off her ass with the cheapest, thinnest, least-absorbent toilet paper money can buy. The paper will be translucent and rip off one square inch at a time. There will be leak-through and you will experience poop on your hands thirty seconds before you're supposed to dive into a meal you paid good money for. You will return to your cold food with zero appetite.

When you return to your table, you will spend the entire meal avoiding the hateful gaze of other patrons as your toddler stares laser beams into their foreheads and speaks loudly about their physical characteristics.

You will ask your waiter for a cup of water for your toddler, and he will return with a full-size glass of ice water with no lid

"My child is perfectly behaved in restaurants and never acts up. Maybe some of you should just take the time to raise better kids."

RESPONSE: "Go fuck yourself."

THE SANCTIPARENT

and hand it directly to your child as a way of saying, "Fuck you for bringing your kid in here."

If you came with a helper in the form of a spouse, one of you will spend your time walking the toddler around the restaurant and outside like he is a cocker spaniel while the other, luckier parent eats alone.

You will do your best to prevent a tantrum, but your child will sense your fear and unleash the ugliest outburst you've ever seen, making you look like an incompetent failure to the entire room.

Overall, you will have wasted $12 on a child entrée of macaroni and cheese that will go uneaten. You will take the macaroni and cheese home and attempt to feed it to your child the next day for lunch to recoup your money. Your child will refuse the macaroni and cheese over and over, and you will end up eating it standing up in front of the fridge three days later.

If, after all of this, you still want to take your toddler to a restaurant, don't say you haven't been warned.

The only time taking your toddler into a restaurant is recommended is if there is a natural disaster and said restaurant is your family's agreed-upon meeting location. Even then, take an iPad.

5

Your
Unraveling
Life

There was a time when your mornings were spent happily burrowing into your sheets until you decided to hop out of bed. You'd leisurely sip a cup of coffee at home or perhaps take a slow walk to the trendy new brunch place to try the buttermilk waffles you'd heard so much about. Aside from rent and basic necessities, your income was mostly disposable. Your evenings were spent laughing with good friends over even better wine. This was your pre-parent life. It's gone now. It's gone forever.

The Cost of Raising a Toddler

Toddlers don't need much in terms of material belongings, but you'll still spend a fortune on them. The bulk of the money will go to paying people to keep them busy. After that, you'll spend money on Pull-Ups, which, if you didn't know, are $18/diaper. I say diaper because that's what a Pull-Up is. Don't kid yourself. Just because the sides are a little more permanent in nature doesn't mean your kid isn't still pissing and shitting himself in a disposable diaper. Pull-Ups cost so much because they sell the illusion that you are that much closer to having a potty-trained kid when in reality you're not closer at all. They're like the Spanx of diapers. Pull-Ups are a lie.

You're going to spend a considerable amount of cashola on toys: plastic outdoor playhouses that click together and cause large patches of your lawn to die underneath, mini seesaws, $5,000 backyard swing sets, play tables, and countless blinking/

flashing toys. Why do you buy them? Because you hope that eventually you'll find that toy that your toddler loves so much that he stays away from you for more than fifteen minutes.

Each toy purchase is a gamble for a moment of peace. Toys are like lottery tickets. You know you're going to lose, but it's fun to try.

Other Costs Associated with Having a Toddler:

- ★ Adult beverages
- ★ Netflix subscription for relaxation purposes
- ★ Antidepressants
- ★ Preschool/childcare
- ★ Replacing broken electronics/mobile phones

- ★ Cleaning supplies
- ★ Repairing gashes on leather couches
- ★ Recarpeting your home
- ★ Monthly car cleanings
- ★ Conditioning treatments for your hair, which is falling out

You will also spend a large amount of your family's income on takeout food. It's easier to deal with meals being constantly rejected when you aren't the one cooking. Plus, The Witching Hour is NOT an ideal time to cook. Your energy is at its lowest and your toddler is at her assholiest. It's much easier to have someone deliver some crappy food than to try to cook with a human puppy hanging off your leg, whining like Bruno Mars.

Toddlers are expensive.

The Destruction of Your Home

Toddlers have no sense of self-preservation and will gladly climb, jump from, and scale objects in your home as if they were Mount Kilimanjaro. They will also attempt to eat coins, put forks in outlets, and hang glide off of dining room tables. Expect to spend every waking second keeping their soul inside their body. You will NOT have time to clean. Even if you do clean, your efforts will be destroyed in a matter of moments, as organized environments go against toddlers' primal natures. Cleaning hurts their sensibilities, which is why as you tidy up they will trail you, destroying your progress. Have you ever noticed that kids take toys out as you put them away? This is no accident. You can hire someone to come in and clean your home, but unless they're willing to live in, your money will be wasted. The one thing small kids are good at is making enclosed spaces look like dumpsters. You can fight it but you will not win.

When you have toddlers, it's normal for your home to look like a tornado of plastic crap, cereal, and mismatched socks. During the toddler years, it is vital that you abandon all hope of having a decent-looking house. Your job is only to keep the child alive and somewhat presentable. Get used to feeling crumbs in your bed at all times.

If your laundry has a permanent place in your home (one third of the couch space), don't be ashamed. Your mother-in-law has made you think that putting away clothes is a real thing, but it's not and she's a damn liar. Get your children accustomed to rifling through piles of clean clothes for their socks.

Tips for Living with Toddlers:

★ Keep the vacuum cleaner out. There's no point in putting it away.

★ Don't own anything made out of glass.

★ Don't have fabric-covered couches unless you love scrubbing out bodily fluids until your fingers are raw.

★ No carpet. Just hardwood. Better yet, try to live in the forest.

★ No sharp edges unless you've always dreamed of having a child with an eye patch.

- ★ Buy enough paper towels to fill a crawl space. Then get six more crates of the stuff.

- ★ All-purpose cleaner. Stock up.

- ★ Disinfecting wipes. You need these. (Poop.)

- ★ Get used to walking on crumbs. Wear socks or slippers or your bare feet will feel like they were dipped in kitty litter.

- ★ Learn to love the sight of dishes piled in the sink.

- ★ Find the view of a living room covered in toys as beautiful as a sunset.

THE SANCTIPARENT

"Not everyone lives in a trash can just because they have kids. My home is orderly and neat because I care. Shame on you."

RESPONSE: "Your home is orderly and neat because the only thing you love more than your kid are Instagram likes. Go eat a bag of dicks."

Toddler Decor

If you have an actual bedroom for your toddler, this is fantastic. Decorate it with Elmo or whatever show he's into. If you're a contemporary parent or blogger, decorate it with hand-painted leaves from your backyard spray-painted gold and framed photos of places you've never been. Make a bed out of a hollowed-out oak tree and Pinterest the shit out of it. Keep in mind that this bedroom will be primarily for time-outs.

The Physical Toll

Besides all the weight you'll gain from drowning your nightly sorrows in takeout and homemade sangria, having a toddler will have physical consequences.

Hair

Mothers, during pregnancy your hair will grow thick and lustrous. After your child's birth, your hair will start to fall out George Costanza–style. During toddlerhood, this will increase. Your hair will also start to prematurely gray from both stress and fear that your life will always suck this hard. For a toddler, a parent taking a shower is a serious offense, so expect your unconditioned hair to become brittle. During the time your child is between one year and four years old, you will look like a broom in yoga pants.

Skin

Because your toddler will have eaten all your lotion, your skin will be at its driest. Since you live on a steady diet of refined sugar, toddler meal scraps, coffee, Red Bull, and alcohol, you will be vitamin deficient. Combined with the salt from the tears you cry at night, this will make your skin resemble the Sahara in the summer: dry, flaky, and sallow. Expect to rock the Disney witch look for at least three years. Pancake makeup would help, but unless you're a Real Housewife, who has time for that?

Nails

It's perfectly normal for your nails to look like you dig graves for a living. It's almost poetic, because at times you will feel as if your toddler is harkening your death.

Clothes

You can always spot the toddler parents. They're dressed for the gym but have no membership. It's important to wear comfortable athletic clothes while caring for a toddler because your day will be a marathon of getting shit for her. You will lose the will to change every day, so just buy two pairs of black yoga pants and rotate them when your partner tells you that you smell like rotten afterbirth.

Shoes

Flats. Only flats. Only an idiot wears heels when taking care of a toddler who may break into a run at any moment. If you need dress shoes for work, carry a pair of cross trainers at all times. Small children can sense when you're at a disadvantage and will use this against you.

Overall Cleanliness

Get used to living with your personal hygiene at an all-time low. You will smell like medical waste. You will smell like a month-old cream of crotch casserole sprinkled with Parmesan testicle cheese. Sometimes the wind will shift and you will catch your own scent and think, "Is there a dead raccoon nearby? Oh wait, that's just my privates."

6

How to Keep Your Toddler Off Your Back

THE SANCTIPARENT

"I love taking my toddler to the park and playing with him. We stay for hours and build castles together. I don't get parents who don't want to be with their kids."

RESPONSE: "You smell like shit."

You need to keep your toddler busy to avoid going stir-crazy. What is stir-crazy? This is when parents leave adult reality and begin to enter their toddler's world. Symptoms include: 1) identifying with cartoon characters, 2) becoming sexually attracted to members of The Wiggles, 3) forgetting what it's like to have a conversation with someone who isn't currently shitting her pants, and 4) eating Goldfish out of the couch cushions.

To avoid this condition, you need to leave your home regularly to keep your child from talking to you too much.

Take Them to the Park

All parents hate taking their kids to the park. We do it to wear them out and give them just enough social interaction to not end up living in our basements twenty years from now.

If you take your toddler to the park regularly and push him on the swings even though what you really want to do is sit on the bench buried in BuzzFeed articles, good for you. You get a gold star for trying. Hell, even if you are buried in a BuzzFeed article or six (they're catchy, aren't they?), you still get a gold star because you haven't abandoned your child and that's how we define success around here.

The Park Sucks. How to Deal:

★ Bring your own sand toys. Toddlers hate sharing, and can you blame them? Sharing sucks. Pony up $6 and invest in some dollar-store plastic shovels and buckets to keep your kid busy. Write your kid's name on them in black Sharpie.

★ Position your kid away from smaller children. Toddlers like to dominate situations but because they're so small and puny, toddlers often find themselves at a disadvantage. When toddlers see a smaller child, they will instinctively want to harm that kid by throwing sand directly in her face or kicking him in the back. This is normal. Avoid a lawsuit and confrontation with police by keeping your toddler away from children who reek of weakness.

★ Position your kid away from other toddlers. Despite being similar in size and weight, toddlers do NOT have an interest in playing together. Think of it this way: Do you like your coworkers? No. You want their lives to fall apart. Toddlers feel the same way about their peers. They engage in what is called "parallel play," which is when they sit close enough to occasionally try to steal each other's shit but don't interact. Do not try to force a toddler relationship on your kid just because you have a parent-crush on another adult. This will be disastrous, as your toddler will be able to sense your interest in another human being and try to sabotage it by spitting at them or slapping you in public. As with any jealous lover, a toddler's endgame is not that you are happy, but that you are isolated and devoted 100 percent to meeting his needs.

★ Take lots of food. Toddlers are foraging beasts. They will happily and greedily follow parents with snacks better than yours. To avoid the humiliation of your toddler begging strangers for food, take at least four juice boxes, a bottle of water, fourteen string cheeses, crackers she's never seen before, a jam sandwich, a large bag of Ruffles potato chips, and two lollipops. You need two lollipops because one is going to be the wrong color. That one is for throwing in the sand.

★ Congratulate yourself on going to the park. Take between 10 and 800 photos to let your Facebook friends know what a fantastic parent you are and how much they suck for being in front of the TV with their kid. Sit close enough to your toddler to prevent her from harming others, but not so close that she can get sand on your phone.

Park Hazards:

★ Water fountain. Don't let your kid drink from the water fountain. By day it's a place to catch a cool, refreshing sip of water, but by night it's a sink where people without permanent addresses take whores' baths. If you feel okay with letting your kid drink water from the same spout where a drug dealer rinses off his junk after receiving oral sex in lieu of payment, be my guest. Have fun filling that prescription for antibiotics. The only thing you should ever use the water fountain for is for playing in the sand. You can't get hand herpes. Go ahead and destroy the sand box by flooding it for your kid. You paid for it with your tax dollars, so it's basically yours.

★ Razor blades. Every now and then you'll hear on the news that some wacko has left razor blades around a park. Look up from your phone every hour or so to make sure your kid has all her flesh. If she doesn't, finish your TMZ article and then call 911 or something. I don't know, I'm not a doctor. Apply pressure if you feel like it. I'm almost positive that fingers grow back anyway. They're like iguana tails.

★ Ice-cream truck. Ice-cream trucks prey on toddlers because their bottom line depends on your little mouth breather crying until you buy a $3 Popsicle that costs ten cents in the store. Some people will tell you that you should lie to your kids and tell them the ice-cream truck plays music when it's out of treats, but that won't work at the park. Herd mentality will kick in and your kid will see other kids stuffing their faces with high-fructose delights. Go ahead and buy the ice cream. Get some soft serve for yourself and drizzle it with amaretto from your hip flask. You don't carry a hip flask? Weird. Get one, then charge other parents a dollar each for a drizzle and you'll turn a nice profit.

★ Annoying neglected kids. There's always that one kid at the park who you can tell hasn't been given affection since the nurse swaddled him on his day of birth. Initially you'll feel sorry for this kid as he follows you and your child around and tries to join in on games. These feelings will turn to annoyance when the orphan won't leave you alone. He'll ask questions, make demands (push on the swing, some of your snack, a warm embrace, etc.), and keep trying to touch you as a way to get in his human-contact quota. The parents of this minor are almost never to be seen. These kids are not homeless, they're usually well-dressed and groomed, but their asshole parents are hoping that the world will do their job for them. Look, it takes a village but at the end of the day, your kid is your motherfucking kid. Handle that shit.

Getting the Hell Out of There

No matter how your toddler behaves at the park, you are required
by law to take her home with you. This is an unfortunate part of
the legal system, one that does not take into consideration the
rights of parents.

Toddlers hate leaving the park. When you arrive they usually
assume that you now live there, so saying good-bye shakes them
to the core. Pack light when you visit the park, or use a backpack,
because you will have to carry your toddler out under your arm
like a newspaper. Try not to pay attention to the looks from other
parents. Move quickly. You will have to force your child's body
into the car seat like you're pushing down the trash. Put some
muscle into it. Don't park your car close enough for anyone to
record your license plate for Child Protective Services. Snitches
are everywhere.

Distract Them with TV

Let's be honest: Without television, most of you would have driven off a cliff by now, Thelma-and-Louise style. We're lucky to live in a time when a babysitter is just a click away. Experts will tell you that screen time is bad for kids, but do you know what else is bad for kids? Getting dropped off at a 7-Eleven with a duffel bag full of clothes. TV will keep you sane. Use it as much as you want. Remember, we set the bar very low around here. Our goal is to make it through the day, not to win trophies.

There are a crapload of options when it comes to entertaining your child with TV. Most television stations geared to toddlers have twenty-four-hour programming or begin at 3:00 a.m. because they know the little bastards love to be up at all hours.

PBS is for parents who want to plop their kids in front of the TV but feel guilty. *Sesame Street* is definitely educational and not completely unbearable. Every once in a while a celebrity will come on and act like they invented happiness, but besides that, it's not bad. However, this network used to broadcast *Caillou* to children so we have to question their judgment.

Whether you choose Nick Jr., Disney, or PBS, the most important thing to keep in mind is that your kid is hypnotized to the point where they stop asking for things.

Netflix is a wonderful option because it allows your kid to watch entire seasons of shows in one sitting. Give your toddler a fresh diaper, cup of milk, and a box of crackers, and look who now has a few hours of alone time? You are winning at this parenting game. Parent Expert Level: UNLOCKED.

The Blacklist

If you're unfamiliar with Caillou, he is the leader of the toddler community. He is the Dark Lord from whom they take orders. Caillou is who every toddler aspires to be. He's a whining shit stain of a kid who, despite having no redeeming qualities, not even physical attractiveness, still gets everything he asks for. If most of us were Caillou's parents, we would have dropped him off at Grandma's house and not looked back. He is a demon's spawn. His whine could strip paint. His cries generate no sympathy in parents, only rage.

Parents, have you noticed that as your child watched *Caillou* he began whining more? If you have not gotten your child addicted to this degenerate of a television-show character, proceed with caution. No animated child in history has angered parents like Caillou has. If you Google his name, you will find images of him walking through flames like a demon and YouTube channels dedicated to discussing his assholery.

Next we'll tackle *Max & Ruby*. This series tells the tale of two bunny siblings. It's never stated outright that the female elder sister, Ruby, killed their parents, but it's implied. The rabbits are now raising themselves with a little financial help from their grandmother. Her silence was bought with threats. The purpose of this show is to teach toddlers how to mentally abuse their friends and family. Ruby treats Max like shit, and I'm 99 percent sure he's going to snap and make a potpie out of her in upcoming seasons. Cannibalism aside, I support his decision. She has it coming. Hopefully he goes full Dexter and takes out Caillou, too.

Handy Manny is also a popular show for youngsters. It's a program featuring Manny, a struggling handyman whose addiction to hallucinogenics is spiraling out of control. Manny is convinced that his tools frequently come alive and argue among themselves. His neighbors take advantage of his decreased awareness to make him work on shit for free.

SpongeBob SquarePants is a show designed to help parents who need a reason to rip out their eardrums. The sound of this character talking and laughing has been the cause of every major world war.

Bubble Guppies is the tale of four or five sperm living in some guy's balls. They sing, dance, and learn lessons.

Buy Shit

Unfortunately, your toddler will probably get bored with her show eventually and want something from you. This is sad, yes, but you can prepare yourself by filling your family room with so many toys that it takes her hours to make her way toward you.

We all say we're not going to be that parent whose living room looks like Chuck E. Cheese threw up in it, but owning a massive number of toys is key to surviving the toddler years. The toys aren't for your kid to play with; they're to serve as stumbling blocks. Keeping your home like an obstacle course will help wear her out. Your house should look like an episode of *Hoarders* but with fewer rat droppings and more colorful shit.

The truth is that kids will play with their toys 8 percent of the time. The other 92 percent of the time they want your iPhone, the remote, Saran wrap, razors, mail, and other household items. The more inappropriate and inconvenient the item, the more they will want to hold it, love it, and call it their own. Don't spend too much money on fancy wooden Waldorf toys when, at the end of the day, your toddler would be just as happy to unwrap tampons for an hour. (Those tampons are still good; don't throw them out.)

Prepare yourself by always having safe trash around for your little mess to take joy in. Fill a trash can with gum wrappers and watch your child's face light up. Paper. Beer bottles. The cardboard boxes McDonald's apple pies come in. Toddlers love that shit. You could dump a box of recyclables over toddlers' heads and they'd be in paradise because the bottom line is: Toddlers love trash.

For your own sanity, never, ever buy toys that talk or sing. There's nothing adorable about hearing a toy say something ultracreepy like, "Sing me a pretty little song" or "I love when you brush my hair" at 2:00 a.m. as you make your way to the bathroom in the dark. You will crap your pants. During the day, toys that emit noise will grate on your nerves. There's a good chance that a well-meaning friend will buy your kid one of these pieces of toy chlamydia. Wait until you're alone and remove the batteries. When your kid grunts in protest, shake your head and look as confused as possible. You can also just throw that shit in the dumpster while he sleeps. Never let your kid see you get rid of them. Toddlers are territorial animals. They are very averse to environment changes. Wait until the middle of the night and put all that crap in a garbage bag. Donate it and let it annoy a family in need.

Hire a Digital Babysitter

If you have an early riser, a tablet will keep her busy while you go back to sleep on the couch. But never, ever download an application that your child needs your help to play. Life is hard enough. Be wary of games that are free upfront but offer in-app purchases. Who in their right mind would pay $3 for animated fruit? You would while half asleep.

Toddlers quickly become addicted to electronic games. This is wonderful because while they're playing they won't be crying at your feet. Limit your little baby's screen time to no more than six hours a day for maximum intelligence. Chances are your toddler will become addicted and start monopolizing your device.

Lies You Can Use to Get Your Phone Back:

★ "Phone has to go night-night." Toddlers don't know that phones aren't alive. Make a bed out of an empty box of condoms and tuck your Samsung in with a Kleenex. Turn off the lights and close the door while holding a finger to your lips and saying *Shhh! Phone sleeping!* Your toddler will be confused as hell.

★ "Phone needs to charge." Toddlers love using up your phone's battery and handing it to you dead, right when you're expecting a call. Every now and then take it from him and put it on a high shelf. Maybe the phone needs to charge, maybe it doesn't. Point is, your toddler won't be touching it with his dirty yogurt-covered hands.

★ "Phone is broken." Toddlers know what broken means because it's their favorite thing to do.

★ "Phone lost." If your toddler wants to play on your phone when you don't want her to, just tell her you can't find it. Stop just short of filing a false police report.

Note: Are you Oprah rich? No? Buy a case for your tablet. This should go without saying. Don't get a cute case with pictures of animals on it; buy the kind that soldiers use—the type that keeps electronics functioning in monsoons and can be dropped out of helicopters. If you don't, your toddler will destroy a $500 piece of hardware in a blind rage over a game not working correctly.

THE SANCTIPARENT

"Multiple studies have shown that screen time for children under two is not advisable and can cause ADD; therefore I prefer to watch cloud formations with my child."

RESPONSE: "My kid loves clouds, too. iCloud. It's where the games are. And she already has ADD: Annoying me every Damn Day. I treat it with screens, so shaddup."

Get Your Pinterest On

The very first craft your toddler does will take place during birth. She will rearrange your vagina into shredded meat. Once you're all healed and your kid is two, people will expect you to start doing crafts involving paper and crayons. This serves no purpose and will not make your child smarter, but it will give you a few photos to post on Facebook.

If you're into crafts, search Pinterest for "easy toddler activities." Chances are a tutorial for handprints in the shape of turkeys or homemade play dough will pop up. Go for it. It will end in your child crying and eating most of that salt dough shit, but at least you'll have photos for when she's older and claims you never did anything with her.

If you're not craftsy, avoid Pinterest during the toddler years. That website is like a frenemy who is kind to your face, but then tells everyone what a slut you were in college (and high school). Pinterest serves only one purpose: to make you feel like a horrible failure of a human being. No person has time to chevron-paint a bedroom, make toddler lunches that look like cartoon characters, or build a sensory table. Have you seen those ice-cube snack trays full of strawberry chunks, blueberries, cracker pieces, and cheese? We all know that those might be cute, but your hyena will flip it on to the floor faster than you can say "failed IUD." Backyard car washes with sponges and tubing . . . Pinterest assumes that you are a cross between June Cleaver, Martha Stewart, and a Home Depot employee, not a tired-ass, cranky parent of a toddler who is just trying to keep the kid entertained for a few minutes.

In conclusion, crafts are overrated and trying to do them with toddlers is what preschool teachers are paid for, so leave it to the professionals.

Hunt Down a Playgroup

If you live in a place where it's next to impossible to meet other parents, join a playgroup. Find your ragtag crew of underachieving misfits within the group. Keep in mind that playgroups usually have rules and expectations. Still, it's a worthwhile sacrifice to bring in the occasional plate of store-bought muffins—you'll avoid sitting alone with your toddler in your living room every day.

Find a Friend

Playdates are not for socializing toddlers; their #1 purpose is to complain with your friends and possibly day-drink a little bit. During the toddler years, support is everything if you want to make it out mentally intact. Find some cool, laid-back people. You'll be able to spot them by their dirty clothes, Popsicle mustaches on their kids, and curse words.

Playdate Conversation Starters

Has parenting a small child left your social skills rusty? Keep this list of friendly talking points nearby and watch the friends roll in!

1. Which of your kids is your favorite so far?

2. If you were a member of the Donner party, which one of your in-laws would you be most eager to consume?

3. What's the earliest you've ever been to McDonald's?

4. I feel like Elsa from *Frozen* was kind of a bitch. Do you agree?

5. How many days are you going on with the same underwear?

6. Were any of your kids accidents?

7. Do you have credit card debt? How much?

8. How many sexual partners have you had?

9. Are you available for surrogacy?

10. What's your favorite color . . . of people? Your favorite race.

11. Do you like picking scabs?

12. Washing your hands after changing a pee pee diaper: Yay or Nay?

13. What's your favorite food to binge-eat?

14. Do you babysit?

Look at you, life of the party!

7

Asshole Parents

It wouldn't be fair to talk about the assholishness of toddlers without talking about their parental counterparts. Toddlers have an excuse when it comes to their shitty behavior: They're learning how to be people. If you're an asshole of a parent, it's all on you.

There are five main types of parents that we all hate. If you're one of these, know that we can't stand you. You might think you have friends, but you don't. You have an audience. We all talk shit behind your back and keep you around for entertainment and because our kids might be friends. Change your ways. It's not too late.

The Overly Competitive Parent

If your Facebook page is all humblebrags, you might be an overly competitive asshole parent. If you are constantly one-upping ("Oh, your toddler is finally talking? Mine just finished *War and Peace*"), you might be an overly competitive asshole parent. For shit's sake. Calm the fuck down about EVERYTHING. This parent believes that her child is an extension of her very fragile ego. Anything can be a sport with this asshole: whose kid is eating the healthiest, whose kid is going to the best school, whose kid is the funniest, whose kid is the cutest, whose kid was born the quickest, whose kid was born with the least amount of white stringy stuff all over their body, you name it. You are a mess of a parent if you're making your child compete in the Parental Olympics 24/7.

The Crazy Crunchy Parent

We get it. The world is teeming with toxins and we're all full of tumors and dying if we don't follow whatever special diet you're on this week. Vaccines are straight bleach, breastfeeding is the only way to go, formula is the devil's semen, regular school is for future dog rapists, plastic bottles will give your kids eye gonorrhea, and you have all the answers. Thank you for the hourly Facebook links from obscure websites that back up your claims. We appreciate it. Thanks for picking apart our meals and lifestyles with your passive-aggressive comments.

Look, we know you're not all wrong, but you make living a natural life look like about as much fun as joining a cult, so we ignore you. P.S. Shut the fuck up.

The Fake Perfect Parent

If you can't share an image of your family online without editing it in Photoshop first, you fall into this category. It really is unnecessary to digitally whiten your three-year-old's baby teeth. This parent is dedicated to sharing her crafts, balanced meals, clutter-free living room, and vacation photos so that everyone knows just how wonderful everything is all the time. Her kid's designer wardrobe cost more than your car. Her favorite hashtag is "#soblessed."

The "This Is Easy" Parent

This parent is one of the worst offenders. His motto is "Isn't this fun?" This parent says annoying things like "Every moment is a gift" and "Oh, well!" God loves this person more than any of us and gave him a very easy, awesome child who loves raw vegetables, sleeping through the night, and being respectful even though you know for a fact that this parent didn't teach the kid these things. "She just came out like that!" is the response this fucker parent gives when you point out that he has a very easy child. Meanwhile your kid is eating sand by the handful at the park. Don't spend too much time with this parent or you might harm him.

Special Little Snowflake Parent

This parent is convinced that their little Daisy or Johnny is not a mere mortal but a deity. You can spot these parents by their endless gushing about how wonderful their spawn is and how everything their kid does or thinks is not only developmentally well above average but genius. If these people could boil down their child's piss and inject it to get high, they would. When you look at their kid, you see a kid; they see Zeus, Poseidon, and all the Greek gods clad in 3T jeans. The only thing these asswipes want to talk about is how gifted their child is and what their child painted last week and how wonderfully he's doing in his baby philharmonic orchestra blah, blah, blah. Don't expect them to show any interest in your rat-faced commoner of a child.

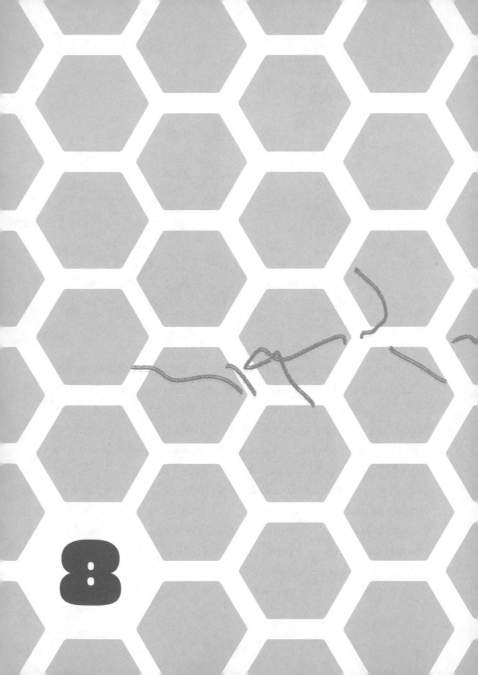

8

Getting Your Toddler to Listen (LOL)

Toddlers don't listen. They can't hear anything above the low drone of their innermost desires. Toddlers, much like show dogs, communicate through reward and punishment. The reason your empty threats don't work is because toddlers are equipped with finely tuned BS-O-Meters. They know when you're lying and act up accordingly.

Common Empty Threats

YOU: *"I'm going to tell your father."*

TODDLER: *"No you won't, you're going to tell Facebook. Do you think I care what your raggedy friends think of me? By the time Daddy gets home, you'll be so thankful to have someone to throw me at that you'll spend the rest of the evening in the kitchen making yourself drinks and forget all about this moment."*

YOU: *"If you do that one more time you're going to be in big trouble!"*

TODDLER: *"If I do this one more time you're going to get so mad that you'll change the scenery. The mall? The park? Starbucks, where you'll get a venti mocha Frappuccino with three extra espresso shots because I woke up at the ass crack of dawn, and I'll get a chocolate cookie the size of my head? Why not."*

YOU: *"Do you want me to call Santa?"*

TODDLER: *"Actually, yes. Tell him that I've already broken all my toys and am going to need fresh ones. You're not kidding anyone—I know Santa is coming no matter what. You love watching me open those presents more than I love playing with them."*

Do you see where we're going with this? Toddlers know you're lying when you threaten them. Talk means nothing to a toddler. They come from the streets. And in the streets, actions mean everything. When dealing with an asshole, you have to put your money where your mouth is. The best we can do is actually put them in a time-out and let them experience the earth-shattering horror that is staying still while the world continues to spin around them. I don't recommend threatening to burn their stuffed animals unless you're going to videotape that shit and send it to me. Burning their toys is cruel. It'd be funnier to stomp the shit out of their LeapFrog tablet *Office Space*-style, but that might land you in some kind of government-mandated parenting class.

Tantrums: When Toddlers Go Apeshit

There is nothing fucking worse than your toddler falling to the ground in a crowded mall and throwing a tantrum. Tantrums can be caused by a variety of reasons: hunger, fatigue, boredom, or just a desire to make you look like a jackass. Everyone has seen toddlers lose their damn mind over the seeds in an orange, someone putting them into their car seat before they were ready, or the sky being an ugly shade of blue.

The best thing you can do when your kid starts to lose her shit in public is to get the hell out as fast as you can. Those threats under your breath aren't going to do jack when your toddler reaches that place of no return where her eyes roll back into her head. Only you know when your spawn has gone to the bad place where she won't be reasonable or respond to your voice. When that happens, get to your car as fast as you can. Knock strangers down if you have to.

Your toddler's biggest weapon during a tantrum isn't her gorilla yells or her crazy thrashing around. It's the audience. Toddlers are assholes, but they're not idiots. They know that by embarrassing the fuck out of you, they increase their chances of getting what they want. By going to your car, forcing them into a car seat, and taking them home, you've removed their source of power: your shame. Let them have a tantrum in the living room. Who cares? Toddler tantrums are a good opportunity for you to catch up on email until that little mofo calms down and is ready to act like a human again. It's not your job to sing "Swing Low, Sweet Chariot" in your child's ear while she screams and tries to slap you in the face.

"Tantrums are a sign that you are not in tune with your toddler. Your child needs emotional healing. Was your child born via C-section by any chance?"

RESPONSE: "I just keyed your car."

You cannot talk a toddler down from a tantrum any more than you can talk a tornado down from destroying lives. When a toddler is going full ape, you get in your storm shelter and wait it out. Tantrums serve one purpose and one purpose alone: to strip your nerves like a wire so that you'll give the toddler what he wants. The more you give in, the more tantrums you'll get, so become good at tuning them out. Learn to distance yourself from reality and find a happy place to reside. Only idiot parents whisper, "Hey, buddy, hey, hey there, hey, little buddy" while their kid loses his fucking mind. He can't hear you. Try reflecting his feelings if you're up for that kind of new-agey bullshit, but no one will blame you if you don't.

10 things

You Thought You'd Never Say

That You Now Say

1. I don't care how hungry you are, we don't lick peanut butter off the sidewalk.

2. What have I told you about biting dogs?

3. I can tell you're pooping because your eyes are watering.

4. We don't put lunch meat in the dryer.

5. Don't scratch inside your diaper and then touch your face. You're going to get pinkeye.

6. Crayons do not belong in your nose. I don't care if you had an itch.

7. Your ears don't get hungry; please stop feeding them.

8. We don't pee on our friends. Even when we're mad, we don't pee on our friends.

9. There is nothing in the bathroom trash for you.

10. If you do that again, I'm canceling Christmas.

How Not to Die Inside

Spending your days and nights with a child who gives you stress headaches can make you wonder if having kids was the worst mistake you ever made. It wasn't. Having kids while not being rich enough to afford a nanny was the worst mistake you ever made.

There are ways to deal with the pain of having a child who makes you want to scream "WHAT DO YOU WANT FROM ME?" repeatedly while hitting your head against a brick wall. No, I'm not talking about self-help books about spirited (i.e., devilish) children or spending more time outside. Keep reading.

Assemble the Night Stash

Alcohol, chips, and candy will get you through the toddler years like a champ. We touched on this in an earlier chapter, but I want to stress the importance of making sure your home is well stocked with these lifesaving items.

Every parent of a toddler needs her own Night Stash. What is a Night Stash? It is a treasure box full of items such as Skittles, Hershey bars, Doritos, and potato chips. Maybe you live in Colorado and your Night Stash contains a blunt or two. We don't judge around here. Do not, I repeat, DO NOT keep these items in the kitchen where your toddler can sniff them out like one of those truffle-hunting pigs.

Keep your Night Stash in a grocery bag in your closet, or in your nightstand if you don't think your toddler will find it.

Do not attempt to restock your stash while grocery shopping with your children. Toddlers can sense deliciousness and will attempt to steal your hard-earned food. Pick up items in secret whenever you can and shuffle them into your bedroom while your hot mess is hypnotized by *Playhouse Disney.*

Consuming Your Night Stash

Although it can be difficult to wait, your Night Stash will taste 99.99 percent better if eaten while your child is asleep. The last thing you want is a toddler wandering into your room when you have a Reese's half-stuffed into your mouth.

Turn to Liquor

Kids know that liquor is off limits, so you're free to partake in their presence with no risk of having to share. Happy Hour generally starts at 5:00 p.m. in the mainstream world, but for parents of toddlers, as long as you know you don't have to drive anywhere, you're good to go whenever.

You know your limits. The good thing about having children present is you're never actually drinking alone. Don't overdo it or you just might end up the subject of a Lifetime original movie, and nobody wants that.

DRINKS RECIPES
for Parents of Toddlers

"WHY ISN'T YOUR DAD HOME YET" SPRITZER

(usually consumed between 5:15 and 6:00 p.m.)

Uncork a nice bottle of cabernet sauvignon. Pour wine into a measuring cup, Tupperware, or an empty, clean margarine container. Sip on the couch while your child tears apart the toys you just put away. For every minute your spouse is late, dedicate a dollar to a future bottle of wine. This drink is best paired with furious text messages like: "What is taking so long?" "Are you circling the block or something?" and "I can't do this anymore."

"IF YOU DON'T STOP WHINING I MAY START SCREAMING" TONIC

Pour 7 ounces of soda water into a stained plastic cup. Add enough vodka to calm you down. This pairs wonderfully with Handi-Snacks. You know, the "cheese"- and-cracker things. Don't bother with the plastic red rectangle knife for spreading. In the comfort of your home, feel free to use your tongue to lick the spread out. Eat eight. Throw a cracker down to your toddler because you're a good parent.

"WHY AREN'T YOU POTTY TRAINED?" FIZZ

In a clean baby bottle, measure 2 ounces of Baileys Irish Cream. The ounce measurements on the bottle are designed to make pouring liquor more accurate. Pour into a coffee mug. Drink straight. Repeat if you want.

OTHER FABULOUS PAIRINGS

MALT LIQUOR................ Lay's potato chips

WHITE WINE .... Warm Tater Tots or McDonald's Chicken Nuggets (sweet and sour sauce)

GUINNESS.................. Slices of buttered white bread or macaroni and cheese

BUDWEISER................ Memories from your old life

GIN.......................... Anger

BACARDI .... Whole milk

SHIRAZ .... Goldfish crackers

CORONA .... Homemade nachos/your child's pizza crusts

SANGRIA .... Dry store-brand cereal and your bitter tears

PABST BLUE RIBBON .... Hot Pockets

SPARKLING WINE .... Macaroni and cheese from the box

THE SANCTIPARENT

"Wow. Alcohol is the answer for your inability to parent. You have a problem."

RESPONSE: "Why the fuck are you still here?"

If you're the cooking type, know that a drink in hand can take the sting out of having to prepare meals for your family. You may also need one while reading books like *The Giving Tree* during bedtime. If you're not familiar with *The Giving Tree*, it is a manual that teaches children how to be selfish little bastards.

The message here is simple: Treat yo self.

Become a Facebook Stalker

Social media will be your #1 source of non-work-related adult interaction. If you are a stay-at-home parent, the people inside your computer whom you haven't seen since high school will be the only adults you communicate with regularly. There's been a lot said about being an "unplugged" parent who is "present" for her children. That's what the nine-month gestation period is for. Now you're allowed to scroll to your heart's content. Don't let anyone make you feel bad. You're in the same room with your child and chances are you're looking up now and again to make sure he's still there. That's parenting.

Facebook will give you a sense of community with people you kind of hate, keep you abreast of all the new and important cat videos, and allow you to vaguely express negative feelings so that people ask if you're okay. Posting photos of your child in whatever corner of your home isn't covered in crap will make you feel better about yourself.

Stop Cooking

There's no polite way to say it: Cooking for children sucks. And cooking for toddlers is the absolute worst. Not only will you be carrying your screaming, whining child during the hardest part of their day (and the most exhausting part of yours) while he begs for snacks, your kid won't eat the meal. It's the definition of adding insult to injury. Most parents wake up already stressed about what they're going to make that night and how many nerves will be fried by threatening their kids into eating it. Forget about that Crock-Pot nonsense. Nobody wants that brown stew mush anyway. Use your large Ziploc storage bags for their original purpose: holding restaurant takeout menus. Yes, this can get expensive, but ordering food is a vacation you can take every night. And when you think of all the money you'll be saving by not using electricity or gas for the oven, these meals practically pay for themselves!

Water saved not washing dishes (use paper plates) $400/year

Dish soap savings from not washing dishes $200/year

Sponge savings from not washing dishes $600/year

Vodka savings from not having to drink your way through dinner $12,000/year

Medical bills saved from avoiding cooking-related accidents/burns $30,000/year

Investing in your local economy by ordering pizza and/or Chinese food nightly .. $millions

Jobs created from getting food delivered .... $billions

You'd be crazy NOT to order dinner!

Note: It's perfectly fine to order the food after your toddler has gone to bed. Just give her a peanut butter sandwich with carrot sticks and a cup of milk. That'll cover most of the food groups.

Send Them to Their Grandparents

Nobody is enjoying your struggle with your little goblin monkey like your parents. Why? Because you were once a little asshole yourself. Your pain is their sacred revenge. Look closely at your parents when your toddler is melting down and you'll see satisfaction in their eyes. "Yes, my precious. Kick Mommy in the face just like she did to me." Someone once said that toddlers and grandparents get along so well because they have a common enemy. You.

Nobody really gets over the toddler phase. Your parents will never admit it, but they hate you a little bit for what you did and take great joy in seeing you lose the battle with your own little hellion. When your toddler is acting like someone with an acute case of I-Don't-Give-A-Fuck-itis in Target, characterized by trying to throw himself out of the cart, just imagine being a grandparent yourself one day. Imagine taking your grandchildren out on a Saturday morning to Toys Я Us and buying them loud electronic toys and filling them up on Mountain Dew/Pop Rocks before returning them home to your former toddler. How glorious will that be to hear her say, "Why can't you listen?" to her own child?

Toddlers love their grandparents with the love of a thousand suns. It is a pure love based on gifts, hugs, a no-rules environment, and candy. Toddlers enjoy making you look like a liar in front of your parents, so don't bother complaining to Grandpa and Grandma about how your pain in the butt is behaving.

"What? Jimmy isn't eating? He eats just fine with me. He just finished a Greek salad with feta and olives and is asking for spanakopita!"

Grandparents only know the sanitized version of their grandchildren because toddlers save their most terrible behavior for the people they live with full-time.

You do not have an ally in grandparents emotionally, but you do in terms of respite. Drop off your toddler with the grandparents as much as you can. You may feel bad about doing this, but you don't have to. Your child is not being as rotten with them as he is with you. He knows better and depends on grandparents as a source of refined carbohydrates and trans fats.

You don't need to warn your parents ahead of time that you will be dropping off their little angel. Simply show up at their house with your toddler for an unexpected surprise visit to "see how they're doing." Wait for your toddler and parent to be engaged in play or conversation and excuse yourself to use the bathroom facilities. Sneak out the back. Leave a garbage bag full of clean diapers, wipes, and enough clothes for three days in the driveway with a $20 bill for expenses (be considerate). Drive away as if you'd just robbed a bank. Turn your phone on silent. When/if you return and they protest, mumble something like "Oh I thought you knew" or start coughing hard until they drop it and ask you if you're sick. Psychologists call this "Me Time."

Stay Positive

While you love your toddler dearly, she will also make you wish you were dead sometimes. This is normal. It's important to try to stay optimistic. Below are a few affirmations to say to yourself in the mirror once your toddler is finally asleep (midnight) and once again in the morning (3:00 a.m.).

Affirmation:

1. I will take revenge when this child is older.

2. One day this kid will have to change my diapers.

3. Kindergarten is coming.

4. Wine is a thing.

5. I can eat all the cereal I want.

6. Boarding schools exist.

7. Some parents have triplets.

8. It could have been triplets.

9. At least I don't have triplets.

10. Triplets.

10

The Guilt-Free Guide to Day Care and Preschools

Working parents or stay-at-home parents who have simply had enough will find themselves wanting to look for day care or preschool for their toddler. A lot of parents feel judged for putting their toddler in day care or preschool. You should never pay attention to the opinion of someone who isn't currently paying your bills. If you need, or just want, to have someone else take care of your toddler while you earn a living or even just take a few minutes to feel normal, that's your right.

Things to Know When Searching for Day Care or a Preschool:

★ When it comes to price, approach it the same way you do a wine list in a restaurant; you want cheap, but not the cheapest. Choose the one second from the bottom.

★ Look for a preschool with bright colors and crafts tables. This tells you that they're committed to bright colors and crafts tables.

★ Definitely find one that serves meals and doesn't require you to pack a lunch.

★ The day-care place should smell kid-bad but not sewer-bad. If it smells like raw sewage, don't send your toddler there (unless they give you a raw sewage–smell discount).

- ★ Ask about their commitment to parental involvement. If they want parents to be involved, don't choose that one. Ain't nobody got time for that.

- ★ Ask them if they have any kind of fund-raisers. If they say yes, get up and leave. Why should you need to fund-raise when you're already paying so much?

Things to Look Out for:

- ★ You DON'T want day care that will let your kid nap for six hours in the afternoon. They're not getting paid to supervise sleepers. They're getting paid to be annoyed by children. All that rest will bite you in the ass come bedtime.

- ★ You DON'T want day care that is staffed with people who will constantly give you parenting advice. There's nothing worse than getting grilled every day about your parenting at pickup time.

- ★ You DON'T want day care staffed by people you seriously suspect hate kids. If they look at your kids the same way you do in the middle of the night, move on.

THE SANCTIPARENT

"Preschool is nothing but baby jail. I would never abandon my child to be raised by strangers."

RESPONSE: "Sleeping Beauty was raised by fairies in the woods, and she has her own shelf in Walmart now."

Preschool Primer

Pre-K has many benefits including socialization, introducing early learning concepts, and keeping your child away from you for several hours at a time. That said, you should prepare yourself for a few things.

ART: You're going to get a lot of arts and crafts sent home. It's going to look mediocre and overwhelm your living spaces. The main use for all this "art" is to kill spiders. You can throw the rest of it away, but don't let your toddler see you. To toddlers, nothing is trash, especially not crap they've scribbled on. You might be thinking, "How many handprints on paper do I have to keep?" If your toddler were in charge, the answer would be "ALL OF THEM." There are thousands of Pinterest boards dedicated to storing and organizing toddler art by medium, plus binders, giant bins in the garage, etc., but what for? You think one day that shit will be worth something? Or that your child will take all that crap to college with her? Keep one or two to prove she had a childhood, frame another for Grandma for the holidays (this gift costs next to nothing), and put the rest at the bottom of the recycling bin. You'll have to smuggle your toddler's art out of the house the way people sneak snacks into a movie theater or drugs into a nightclub. Get creative. Between the boobs, in your boots—do what you have to do.

SNACK DUTY: You will be asked to bring in the occasional meal. Pay attention to any allergy notices. While it's fine to be lazy, it's not cool to do it at another kid's expense. If you can't make a peanut-free cupcake, then break a $20 and go buy some. Take in a premade grocery-store fruit plate. Do not let overachieving parents make you feel bad for not creating multicolored rainbow piñata cookies with M&Ms on the inside. Even if you did have time, why would you waste it making treats that will literally turn into toddler shit a few hours later, when you can watch Netflix or take a well-deserved nap?

MULTIPLE PERSONALITIES: Your toddler will have a day-care personality and a home personality. The day-care personality will be better because he knows 100 percent that you won't murder him for his bad behavior but the same can't be said for his teacher. Toddlers are smart animals; they know that if they pulled the shit they do at home their teacher might snap. When your toddler's day-care teacher says stuff like "Leo is such a good kid!" and you know Leo is rotten to the core, don't challenge her or try to prove her wrong, because that just makes you look crazy. Yes, Leo woke you up this morning by straddling your head and pissing in your face, and yes, when you were rifling around for your cell phone in your handbag you pulled out a turd Leo had put in there, but just let it go.

Note: One terrible aspect of preschool and day care is that it will put you in direct contact with parents who are doing better than you are. During drop-off and pickup, you will notice that there are parents who drive very expensive vehicles and are physically attractive, fit, and well-dressed. We call these people punk bitches (applies to males and females) and avoid them. If it helps, imagine that their personal life is in shambles.

Look for the parents who look like they were just released from prison: unshaven, hunched over, afraid of sunlight, con-fused, shoes on the wrong feet, etc. These are your people.

How to Pay for Preschool

Preschool is damn expensive. It would be better if it cost an arm and a leg than actual money, because then you'd be able to get two kids through before you were left without appendages. Most families cannot afford preschool but put their kids in it anyway and just try to not cry when the overdraft fees start rolling in.

10 Ways to Make Extra Money:

1. Turn tricks.

2. Sell the gold in your fillings.

3. Become a webcam sex-object person.

4. Sell scrap copper you find in your neighbor's garage.

5. Sell blood plasma.

6. Start cutting hair in your kitchen. If you don't know how to cut hair, make sure you get paid up front.

7. Don't pay and just show up to preschool and drop your kid off. You'll only get away with this for two to three days.

8. Become a wet nurse.

9. Eat Hamburger Helper for dinner every night (don't use hamburger).

10. Get some dirt on the preschool director and blackmail your way in, tuition-free.

Dear Asshole Whisperer,
My kid has a fever. Can she still go to preschool?
—Mom in Vermont

Dear Mom in Vermont,
That depends. Will you get fired if you don't go to work?
Yes? She can go to preschool. Give her some Tylenol. If
they call you, pretend you didn't know. Kids in day care
are sick pretty much 24/7, building up their immune
systems. If you keep your kid home every time he feels
like a cinnamon bun fresh out of the oven, he'll miss more
days than he'll actually attend. If your snowflake is barfing
up his guts, lethargic, and has turned a shade of pea green,
you might want to call in to work.

Dear Asshole Whisperer,
There is a biter in my kid's preschool class. What should I do?
—Dad in North Dakota

Dear Dad in North Dakota,
Teach your kid to bite back. Let your kid know that in
your house you don't start fights, but you always finish
them. If your kid is the biter, file down his teeth.

Dear Asshole Whisperer,
Why does preschool cost so much?
            —Mom in Wyoming

Dear Mom in Wyoming,
Would you want to be a preschool
teacher? 'Nuff said. Having to put
twenty kids down for a nap is going to
cost you. Plus having to wipe the butts
of other people's children probably sucks.

Dear Asshole Whisperer,
Should I feel bad about putting my kid in day care?
            —Mom in Tennessee

Dear Mom in Tennessee,
No. Do what you need to do in life. Haters gonna hate.
Speculators gonna speculate. Live ya life.

THE GUILT-FREE GUIDE TO DAY CARE AND PRESCHOOLS

11

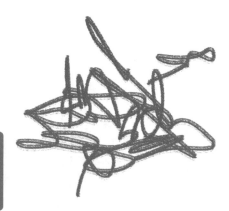

Sleep Drama

123

You thought sleep problems ended with newborns?
That's funny. Welcome to Hades.

Parental Fatigue: How to Deal

Most toddlers wake up at the butt crack of dawn. Combine that with the fact that they keep you in a heightened state of awareness due to their assholery, and you've got a really tired parent on your hands.

There's no simple way to deal with the fatigue of having an Energizer Bunny in OshKosh running around your house. The first thing you can do to help yourself is to get a simple coffee machine. Find one like a Keurig or Tassimo that requires you only to push a button to get liquid energy. Espresso machines and machines that require you to put stuff in filters are way too much to deal with when you can barely remember what day it is. On average, most models cost $100, which is a small price to pay for not falling asleep at the wheel.

Chances are that you won't actually remember to drink your coffee. You'll probably find it in the microwave at 5:30 p.m. when you're heating authentic breaded chicken morsels.

It is essential that you find ways to lie down during the day. If you're at work, find a storage closet or curl up under your desk. If you have an office to yourself, let everyone know that you have a very important conference call, shut the door, and pass out on the floor.

Smart parents find ways to relax while their toddlers are awake. How do you do this? Simple. Make it a game.

Create games that involve lying down and doing nothing. This is key to surviving long afternoons with a small kid. Give these "activities" creative names that make it clear to your child that while you are physically present, you will not be moving or making eye contact.

Games for Tired Parents:

- ★ Sleeping Daddy
- ★ Hospital Invalid
- ★ Tiger with a Problem
- ★ Disinterested Friend
- ★ Sick Person with Eyes Closed
- ★ Broken Worm
- ★ I'm a Blanket

- ★ Quiet Mountain
- ★ Dead Starfish
- ★ Play Around Me
- ★ Mommy Is a Rock
- ★ Friend with Mono
- ★ Pretend I'm Invisible
- ★ Strand of Hair

Buy your toddler a $10 doctor's kit from a toy store and let her tap on your knees and listen to your elbow with the stethoscope. Give her a washcloth, slotted spoon, and some lotion and just let her do random shit to you while you pretend to be somewhere else. Long toddler talons are fantastic for back scratching. Teach her to be useful. Close your eyes. You might fall asleep, so be careful. If you should doze off, when you wake up your bag will be dumped out and your kid might be eating nail-polish-and-drugstore-coupon sandwiches.

Maximizing Naptime

Toddlers must nap. They simply must. The time your toddler spends unconscious during the day will make the difference between your being sane and losing your mind and running through the center of town nude, screaming prophecies.

If you can get your toddler to nap twice, great. If your toddler can only nap once, that's fine, too. She doesn't even need to sleep. "Quiet Time" while your toddler sits in her crib and thinks about life (i.e., yells and kicks the wall) also works. Most people start their toddler's nap after lunch, say 1:00 p.m. A nice 1:00 to 3:00 p.m. nap will change your life. You need the break. Don't try to get anything done, lest the nap schedule look like this.

Nap Schedule for Overachievers:

1:00 P.M. Get toddler to sleep.

1:15 P.M. Do dishes.

1:35 P.M. Pick up family room.

1:50 P.M. Wipe down surfaces.

2:00 P.M. Start a load of laundry.

2:10 P.M. Clean up bedroom.

2:30 P.M. Attempt to figure out dinner. Throw some random stuff in Crock-Pot.

3:00 P.M. Feel good about everything you did and think, "Ahhh. Now to relax for a moment. I deserve it."

The second your ass touches the couch or your head hits your pillow, a sensor will go off in your child's brain and she will immediately wake up crying. Do you see what happened here? You tried to accomplish things and it came back to hurt you. Never forget. Here's what you should have done:

Nap Schedule for Slackers (You):

1:00 P.M. Get toddler to sleep.

1:05 P.M. TAKE OFF PANTS AND GET INTO BED.

1:07 P.M. Netflix and food in bed.

1:10 P.M. Fall asleep with a mouthful of shredded cheese.

3:00 P.M. Hear toddler and get up. Put pants back on.

Is your house clean? No. But do you feel like listing your child on Craigslist? Also no.

Do the right thing. Fall asleep with food in your mouth and no pants. Cleaning during downtime is for suckers and chumps.

The Witching Hour Explained

Toddlers wake up from their naps like angry drunks: confused, belligerent, and emotionally abusive. We call the time period between the "wake up" and "finally asleep" periods The Witching Hour. Don't let the name confuse you, The Witching Hour does not last a mere sixty minutes. It lasts *the rest of the day.*

The Witching Hour is characterized by your child's aggressive whining and not allowing you to put him down.

Alternate Names for The Witching Hour:

★ Why Is This Happening?

★ Grandma, Can You Come Over?

★ I've Lost My Will to Accomplish Things in Life.

★ Parenting Is Killing My Soul.

If you're the working parent to a stay-at-home spouse, this is why you need to rush home at the end of the day. Should you dawdle, you may find your toddler alone in a playpen with a bowl of crackers and a sippy cup of tap water. All that will remain of your spouse is a note on a table saying, "I told you to hurry. Bye."

During The Witching Hour, dinner prep will be next to impossible. If you're truly committed to putting a meal together, invest in a toddler carrier at some point and strap that kid to your back. Or don't and order takeout. Dinnertime will, as always, be hell as your child struggles with wave after wave of fatigue and having to eat something other than cereal.

Common Parental Witching Hour Behavior:

★ Spending your family's life savings on Etsy

★ Sobbing

★ Indulging in a backyard cigarette

★ Filing for divorce online

★ Cursing at your child under your breath

★ Engaging in "angry cleaning"

★ Saying you need to take out the trash and just lingering in the alley next to your house for an hour

* Pretending to use the bathroom and playing on your phone while sitting on the toilet

* Hiding from your family behind boxes in the garage

Surviving Bedtime

Putting a toddler to sleep is kind of like getting that one friend who has had too much to drink out of the bar and home. You spend a lot of time talking softly but sternly about how she needs to stop crying and just do what you say. You might have to clean up her pee or vomit. You listen to her talk about bullshit nonsense. She needs hugs. You get her a lot of water. You sit with her for a while and listen to her get stupidly philosophical. She asks for more drinks and you'll have to tell her "NO." She requests a meal. She tells you she loves you and asks if you love her. She wants to talk about every boo-boo she's ever gotten. At the end of it all, you're exhausted and wonder why your friend can't get her life together.

The difference between your encounter with your intoxicated friend who still hasn't learned that tequila should never be mixed with wine and the bedtime routine is that the latter will have to be done *nightly*.

Despite knowing that night arrives literally like clockwork, toddlers seem surprised that bedtime keeps happening. They approach the event with sadness, rage, and some truly fucked-up behavior. Many of them get diarrhea of the mouth and ask a series of essay questions designed to keep you their hostage. Others begin complaining about bug bites that healed months ago or blanket problems. Some just cry. Some are escape artists who use nightfall as an opportunity to reenact *The Shawshank Redemption.*

I have no advice for you other than to just press forward. Eventually your kid will pass out. You might also pass out in their little Elmo toddler bed.

To prepare yourself for the anguish that is putting a toddler to bed, I've compiled a list of common toddler bedtime stalling techniques.

100 Things Your Toddler Will Say at Bedtime:

1. My favorite toy is in the car.

2. My favorite toy is in the backyard.

3. My favorite toy is at the store and I don't own it yet. Can you buy it online?

4. My blanket is too hot.

5. My blanket is too cold.

6. My blanket is too scratchy.

7. My blanket smells like pee.

8. My pajamas are too big.

9. My pajamas are too small.

10. My pajamas are the wrong color.

11. The pajamas I need are in the washing machine.

12. I'm hungry.

13. I'm thirsty.

14. My hair hurts.

15. My finger hurts.

16. My toe hurts.

17. My mouth hurts.

18. My teeth hurt.

19. My butt hurts.

20. My eyelashes feel weird.

21. I feel sick.

22. Can you read me another story?

23. Can I have one more kiss?

24. Can I have one more hug?

25. Can you change the color of the moon?

26. What if Elmo is my real dad?

27. Who are you?

28. What are we doing tomorrow?

29. Are we poor?

30. What's your maiden name?

31. What's my Social Security number?

32. What country do we live in?

33. Am I adopted?

34. Are you adopted?

35. I want to live with Grandma.

36. Why does your face look mad?

37. Why does your face look so old?

38. Why does your face have lines?

39. What happens when we die?

40. Can I take another bath?

41. Will you make me some popcorn?

42. How come your breath smells like beer?

43. Does Sid the Science Kid have ADD?

44. What's your favorite color?

45. Do you want to build a snowman?

46. What's the opposite of hair?

47. Why is pee yellow?

48. Why is pee warm?

49. Can you get me different socks?

50. Can we change my pajamas again?

51. I'd like new sheets; can we change the sheets?

52. Can I have an orange?

53. Should I take my vitamins now?

54. How did I get here?

55. How are babies made?

56. Am I a robot?

57. Why do we need underwear?

58. Is poop made of chocolate?

59. Why is poop the same color as chocolate?

60. Do we have any chocolate?

61. Is tomorrow my birthday?

62. When is my birthday?

63. What am I getting for my birthday?

64. What color is my cake going to be?

65. Can you tickle my back?

66. Can you tickle faster/ better?

67. How come you're falling asleep?

68. What is grass?

69. How many kinds of animals are there?

70. What are clouds made out of?

71. Have you ever been in a spaceship?

72. What is blood?

73. Can I watch TV?

74. Can I play on the iPad?

75. Can I go downstairs with you?

76. Can I sleep in your bed?

77. Can I have a sandwich?

78. Can I have some chocolate milk?

79. Is tomorrow Halloween?

80. Can I wear a Halloween costume right now?

81. Why are you crying?

82. Are you a goblin?

83. Am I royal?

84. What's 3 + 3?

85. Why?

86. Are you an Elsa or an Anna?

87. Can I fly?

88. Do I have any latent powers?

89. What is a balloon?

90. Are you sleeping?

91. Can I just have a small snack?

92. Cheese?

93. Cracker?

94. Okay, an apple?

95. Can I finish my dinner now?

96. What's for breakfast?

97. What time is it?

98. Are you sleeping again?

99. Where are you going?

100. Can I have one more hug?

This is your life.

12

Potty Training: When the Shit Hits the Fan

Is your toddler still wearing diapers? Who cares. Look at the bright side: At least you're not doing a mountain of pee-soaked laundry from potty training. Even if you never manage to potty train your kid, you can trust that the shame of rolling up to community college in Pull-Ups will take care of that problem for you.

Potty training is either a hellish experience or a piece of cake. There is no in-between. Toddlers either take to it like they were never in diapers (15 percent) or fight the potty like it is their sworn enemy (85 percent). There is no way to know which kind of toddler you'll have. They decide among themselves months in advance. If you have an easy toddler, don't think it has anything to do with you. Anyone with more than one kid can tell you that you were just dealt a good hand, so quit it with the high-and-mighty Facebook posts, ya bitch.

You can buy all the Pull-Ups (the nicotine patch of diapers), cloth training pants, sticker charts, M&Ms, and Skittles you want, but what you really need to prepare for potty training is laundry detergent, because you're gonna be washing. A lot. Make sure you have a bucket, mop, bleach, and towels that you don't mind using on butt nuggets and urine.

Potty training a toddler turns you into a twenty-four-hour janitor. I hope you like shaking wet turds out of a plastic potty and into the toilet, because this will be your life for a while. Keep your nails short and your hair out of your face. This is not a joke.

"I don't believe in potty training. We practiced a combination of elimination communication and 'scooping' wherein for six months I cupped my hands under my child's genitals to lovingly catch the emissions."

THE SANCTIPARENT

RESPONSE: "Remind me never to eat in your home."

Keep some Vicks around and smear that shit under your nose if you have a strong gag reflex.

Potty training means that you will visit every single public restroom in your city. You will experience the joy that is a urine-soaked car seat. You will ponder skipping potty training altogether and just settling into the idea that you will have a fourth-grader in Huggies.

Don't rush potty training lest you become one of those parents who has to bear the shame of regression. Sure, tell everyone that your eighteen-month-old is "fully trained." Just wait until that sucker turns two and you're buying Pull-Ups again. Those feelings of superiority will nose-dive faster than a postpartum woman's sex drive.

Potty-Training

Drinking Games

It isn't all bad, though. You can easily make potty training into a game. Not for the kid, for you.

★ Take a drink whenever your toddler takes a shit on the floor five seconds after you've picked him up from the potty where he was sitting for half an hour.

★ Take a drink whenever your toddler screams that she urgently has to use the bathroom when you're in the grocery store line, airport security line, or the Department of Motor Vehicles line.

★ Take a drink whenever your toddler needs to pee in a place with no restroom, forcing her to urinate between parked cars or behind a bush.

★ Take two drinks if your toddler pulls a used tampon out of the sanitary-napkin metal disposal bin and asks, "Why is this kite bleeding?"

★ Take a drink every time you pick up a Tootsie roll with your bare hands.

★ Take a drink every time your toddler pees on you, soaking you in her people juice down to your skin.

★ Take two drinks for every ten loads of laundry you do.

★ Take a drink every time your toddler pisses himself in public and refuses to acknowledge it.

★ Take a drink every time your toddler shits her pants and casually shakes the turd out of her pant leg.

★ Take four drinks every time you think you're done with potty training when you're really not.

★ Take a drink every time a "friend" tells you that her child was potty trained at six months old and then clock them in the face for lying.

Life can be fun.

13

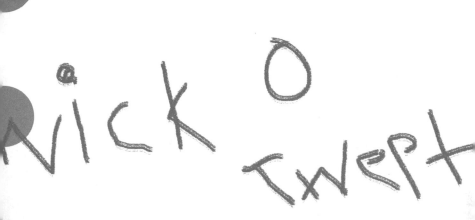

Holiday Guide

145

Holidays help make up for the difficulty of having toddlers. They help you remember why you had children in the first place: photo opportunities.

Halloween

On this magical night, you get to dress your toddler as an idiot and parade him around town. It's your right. As the parent of a toddler, you also have the opportunity to replenish your Night Stash (see page 102) for free.

1. Teach your toddler to say "Twick o Tweet" in the cutest voice he can muster. Not "trick." TWICK. Switching the *R* for a *W* will net you 20 percent more deliciousness to consume while watching *The Late Show.*

2. Invest in an adorable costume like a chicken, dog, or any kind of animal. Stay away from "hipster chic" costumes like band members, food, and dead people. This isn't the time to impress people; it's the time to get free food. The cuteness factor greatly affects how much candy your toddler will be given.

3. Leave the house at around 5:30 p.m. Any earlier than that and people will be hesitant to dig deep into their candy supply. They'll be in early-evening rationing mode.

4. Don't go to malls. Go door to door. If you live in squalor, drive to a nicer community. Look for well-maintained lawns, sculptures, and fountains. The full-size Snickers bars will be worth it.

5. Bring a 10-gallon bucket, baby bath, or heavy-duty trash bag with you, but keep it in the car. I'll explain this later.

6. Start trick-or-treating. Make sure your toddler says his "Twick o Tweet" in a sweet voice and "Thank you." Stand behind him and smile as if you love your family.

7. When your candy bag is half full, go back to your car and dump it into your "trash" bag or baby bath. Repeat until your child can no longer walk. Allow your toddler 5–6 Skittles for energy to get through an additional 6–7 neighborhoods.

8. Within a few hours, you will have a large stash of candy in the trunk of your car courtesy of your little one. And you thought toddlers weren't good for anything?

Thanksgiving

Ah, yes. The holiday of gratitude. What you'll be most grateful for is that it's the one day of the year where it's perfectly acceptable to begin drinking before noon. The average Thanksgiving feast includes a turkey, mashed potatoes, gravy, a bowl of cranberry mess that looks like blood clots, green bean casserole, sweet potatoes, and stuffing. If you're lucky, your toddler will eat the butter off of a roll. Maybe some pumpkin pie crust if she's going through a growth spurt and feels particularly hungry. Most likely, she will request an Eggo waffle. Don't get depressed if your child doesn't appreciate the meal you slaved over, because that's what Instagram is for. Just enjoy the ambiance and hope your toddler doesn't repeat any of the terrible things you've been saying about your relatives all year.

Christmas

Look, don't go all crazy getting your toddler expensive presents. You could wrap up items she already owns and your kid would be delighted. Toddlers just like to unwrap shit. It reminds them of destroying. Wrap plastic cups from your pantry, rawhide, spoons, a Ziploc bag of leaves, a quart of milk . . . whatever you have. You don't need money to make Christmas special for your toddler. Toddlers do not care.

The best part of Christmas is using Santa to threaten them. If you're doing it right, Santa should sound like a cross between a sniper and the NSA: Someone who is always watching them and ready to take serious, permanent action. Let them know that Santa will not let emotions get in the way of burning all their gifts should they disobey.

We need to talk about the Elf on the Shelf. It can be tempting to buy one of these enchanted dolls to control your toddler's behavior. But if your toddler isn't afraid of you, what makes you think he's going to respect a snitch? Second, parents of toddlers can barely remember to brush their own teeth every day, much less put a wooden toy in a zany position every morning. Do yourself a favor, if you're going to buy one of these fools, tell your kid that it only moves when she's bad. If she doesn't listen, the Elf will come into her bedroom and watch her sleep. Problem solved!

Chanukah

Eight nights of gifts sounds harmless until you consider the fact that toddlers believe that anything that happens twice will continue indefinitely. Jewish parents need to prepare themselves for chaos on night nine. Your child will be shocked that the presents and jelly doughnuts aren't a regular thing. You spend enough money on your toddler year-round; feel free to phone this one in. Consider divvying up one large gift to last the entire holiday.

Chanukah Gift Suggestions:

★ An eight-count box of crayons. One crayon per night.

★ An eighty-count box of diapers. Ten diapers per evening.

★ An eight-count box of granola bars.

★ Eight individual Band-Aids.

★ Four pairs of socks. One per evening.

Important Note: Nothing brings a community together like a house fire, but it can be costly. If you're going to have a menorah with a toddler around, use the electric version.

Birthdays

No doubt you're going to want to throw a birthday party for your toddler despite the fact that he will spend the entire event crying. Keep it simple, but not so simple that people feel cheated out of their gifts. Hot dogs, fruit, vegetables, hamburgers, and a store-bought cake are enough. Open a couple of large bags of chips and dump them into a plastic bowl. Buy disposable cups, plates, and napkins. Throw candy at the kids. Quit with all this Pinterest shit. Remember, this is a birthday party, not a fucking wedding. Since when does a birthday party for a baby need an elaborate theme and a corresponding website? Birthdays are a celebration of being that much closer to putting the toddler years behind you.

Birthday Presents: A Guide for Attendees

Congrats on being invited to a toddler's birthday party! I know you'd much rather spend your day sitting on a couch with a glass of wine in hand and no pants, but if you don't go, the parents will silently hate you for life. Don't forget to take a prezzie.

If you give a friend's toddler one of those "corn popper" devices that you push on the floor, the ones that sound like a drive-by shooting, consider yourself an enemy. Your parent friend will just be biding his time, waiting for you to have a kid of your own. One day when you least expect it, he'll give your child something truly obnoxious, like a set of kazoos or a caffeinated lollipop. Don't play this game. Everybody loses.

Don't give paints unless you're also going to host the painting party in your home. For the love of everything holy, do not give a toddler one of those play dough kits. Cleaning dried salt dough out of toy crevices, carpet, and the gaps in wooden floors is a bitch. Age-inappropriate gifts like Rainbow Looms will be burned immediately.

If you don't have any money or common sense when it comes to presents, don't bring one. The kid probably has enough crap anyway.

Your
Nonexistent
Sex Life

If you have a toddler, you probably aren't trying to have another kid. Or maybe you are, because pain is just your thing. In addition to your chemical or latex birth control, nature has also provided ways to keep yourself from reproducing during this trying time.

THE "CHECKED-OUT WORKING DAD" METHOD Coming home and hiding in the bathroom or garage while your loving partner makes dinner with a toddler crying under her feet is a very effective birth control method. It guarantees that no sexy time will be had. The only thing that will go down regularly in your life is the sun. Oh, you need alone time? Chances are your spouse doesn't even know what the fuck that is anymore. When you get home, wash your hands, go pee, wash them again, change, and jump right into the madness you helped create. Alone time. You think this is a motherfucking game? If you ever want to get head again, pull your weight. The quickest way to get cut off from naked Twister is to act like working outside the house makes you exempt from equal parenting. Mofo.

THE "DAMAGED PSYCHE STAY-AT-HOME FATHER" APPROACH Most likely your toddler has already broken your spirit. Being a stay-at-home dad is no joke. Oftentimes, the moms and nannies at the park treat you like a potential sex offender at a time when adult conversation is critical to your emotional health. If you're anything like the stay-at-home dads I know, your libido has been trampled into the carpet like a stale Goldfish cracker and you have no desire to add to your brood. Your best bet is to find some cool stay-at-home dads who get your life. Start a blog. Get on Tumblr and find .gifs that accurately express your pain. You'll have plenty of time at night to create your digital diary now that you're not getting it on.

THE "FML WORKING MOM" TECHNIQUE Undoubtedly, you miss your toddler during the day, but no one will think badly of you if you also admit that after a long day of dealing with terrible bosses and even worse coworkers, the last thing you want to do is argue about broccoli with someone younger than most of your moles. The sheer exhaustion from balancing (and sometimes being judged for) an outside-the-house job is enough to pause ovulation.

THE "I REEK STAY-AT-HOME MOM" BARRIER The stench that comes from your innermost crevices because you haven't showered all week will repel your sexual partner. Which is good, because after an entire day spent being groped by a toddler, sex will be about as appealing as a hummus Popsicle.

Sex: Overcoming the Hurdles

If you do opt to engage in sexual relations while being the parent of a toddler, know that you'll have some hurdles to jump over.

Hurdle #1: The Smell

The smell. I just want to take a minute to reach out to the good people at Febreze. Why have you not developed a spray that makes privates smell like wildflowers? You've done such a good job making junkyard homes smell clean, it's time to toss parents a bone here and make some kind of body spray that serves as a "shower in a bottle." Feel free to use that slogan.

Because they lack the time and will to shower, one or both parents of a toddler will walk around looking relatively normal, but the inside of their underwear will smell like a dive bar–bathroom urinal cake. Since sex tends to expose these crevices, the love den will take on the odor of an outhouse, which doesn't exactly make for a sultry environment.

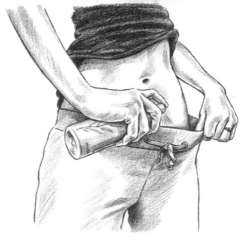

Solution: Have sex with the windows open. Don't turn on any fans, which will just waft the odors directly into your nose. Keep a candle lit to burn off ass/vagina/penis vapors.

Hurdle #2: Fatigue

Fatigue. You're tired as hell from pulling nickels out of your toddler's mouth and scraping perfectly good food into the trash. The last thing you want to do is assume the position. Also, when you've had a small child crawling all over you all damn day, holding your hand, sitting in your lap while you eat dinner, the last thing you want is another person all up in your business. By the end of the day, parents who hang out with toddlers during daytime hours will not want anyone breathing near them. If you dealt with annoying people at work all day, came home to the chaos that is now your life, and then had to do the bedtime routine, you will be too tired to remove your underwear.

Solution: Masturbation! Just kidding. There is no solution.

THE SANCTIPARENT

"I have perfect harmony in all my relationships. How sad for you! Making love is my favorite thing to do!"

RESPONSE: "That's what your mom said last night."

Hurdle #3: Your cock-block toddler.

Toddlers hate knowing that you have relationships that don't include them. They are experts when it comes to sibling prevention. You've probably noticed by now that just as you're feeling frisky and have convinced your partner to drop his or her undies, your little one, who you thought was asleep, lets out an Adam Levine–style falsetto note.

Solution: Turn off the baby monitor so you can't hear your child's cries. This could backfire terribly, so use at your own risk. If your toddler sleeps in your bed, you have no choice but to get it on in the living room or backyard. Hopefully you have a high fence.

If your toddler is in a crib that he can't get out of and you do decide to play through, more power to you. Just make sure you have a lock on your door lest you look up from your passionate gorilla lovemaking to see a two-foot-tall human curiously staring at the business side of your private parts. There's no unseeing that, and it will end up being relayed in great detail to a preschool teacher the next day.

Hurdle #4: Television

Between Netflix, HBO, and basic cable there are so many ways to zone out and forget that you've lost your zeal for living. Staring at a screen while shoving popcorn into your mouth faster than you can chew is so much easier than carving out an intimate moment with your other half. Don't let the boob tube (no pun intended) destroy your sex life. Television may be entertaining, but your partner is your heart and soul.

Solution: Multitasking! Combine the love you have for your shows with the like you mostly still have for your better half. Flip your bedroom television (you should have one) to the channel of your choice and turn up the volume. Assume a sexual position that allows you to face the TV or at least see it out of the corner of your eye. If your partner wants to watch something else, put a laptop or propped up tablet loaded with his legally downloaded programs on your marriage bed. To avoid a conflict/distraction, invest in a pair of earbuds for the party using the portable device.

Beautiful. <3

15

Rites of
Passage

There are certain rites of passage that are universal to the parents of toddlers. Each time you experience one, know that you've earned a badge in the "Parents of Toddlers Scouts of the World" organization.

"DIAPER BLOWOUT SO BAD YOU HAVE TO THROW AWAY AN ENTIRE OUTFIT, SHOES INCLUDED, AND POSSIBLY BURN YOUR CAR SEAT" BADGE.

This one isn't for the faint of heart. Nobody knows what causes poop like this to explode from a toddler's tiny rectum in such massive quantities. Was it the eight apples he ate the night before? Was it Aunt Shirley's potato salad? Is the child possessed by the souls of the damned? There's no way of knowing. All you know is that you can't subject your washing machine to this horror and you will probably never again eat anything resembling yellow curry.

"WHERE THE HELL IS THE OTHER SHOE?" BADGE.

You're pushing your toddler's stroller down a busy street and look down to see that one of her $80 PediPeds is missing. What? How can this be? My child notices when I remove a single Cheerio from her bowl. How did she not notice she's missing a shoe? You look your toddler in the eye and suddenly, from her steely gaze, you realize that she did notice. She did. And she said nothing. You learn an important lesson that day as you retrace your steps, desperately trying to find the lost item (you will never find it).

You've learned that not only can the toddler not be trusted, she gives zero fucks. Not today, not any day.

"THERE'S SHIT IN THE TUB" BADGE. Perhaps you brought your phone into the bathroom. Maybe you just got lost in your thoughts after a long day. Whatever it was, you didn't notice your child's face tense up as he pushed out a Lincoln log under the bubbles. Do you remember what first alerted you? Was it the cloud of brown? Or your toddler's shout as the sea biscuit began floating its way over to him? Either way, you probably screamed and your mind raced. The first reaction is always denial: "No! Baths are for getting clean! Why? WHY?" At one point you knew what you have to do, and you faced this decision with the bravery of the thousands of parents who have gone before you. We don't care what you used to scoop it out. A Lego. A fishing net. Your hand. You did it. You got through it. You can survive anything now.

"THAT WAS THE WORST NIGHT OF MY LIFE; I FEEL LEGITIMATELY TRAUMATIZED" BADGE. This night is hard to describe, but you'll know it when it happens. It starts like any other evening, except your child never sleeps for more than twenty-five minutes at a time and there's no clear reason why. You'll have gotten out of bed so many times that at one point you decide to take your own sleep off the table entirely. The next day will be a haze. You'll feel hungover, betrayed, angry, and scared.

You will eat your emotions. You might burn sage in your child's room to drive out bad energy/evil spirits. One thing is for sure, though: You'll never again be the same.

THE "MY CHILD JUST SLAPPED ME IN THE FACE" BADGE. It happens to everyone. If you're lucky, it happens in the privacy of your own home. If you're unlucky, you're at a family party surrounded by judgmental relatives. Either way, the sting is felt both in your heart and on your cheek as your angry toddler clocks you across the face with an open hand. You're stunned. Frozen. You don't know what to do. Your first instinct is to hit back, but you remember that this person, this individual that hit you, is a child. Your child. When you return to your senses, you struggle to come up with an appropriate response. Time out. A firm talking to. But you're only half present. The rest of you is wondering how, wondering why, the beautiful child you brought into the world, and lovingly cared for up until this very moment, could treat you with such stone cold disrespect. Welcome to toddlerhood.

THE "I JUST CAUGHT VOMIT IN MY HANDS TO AVOID IT HITTING THE FLOOR" BADGE. This badge is earned through instinct. No sane person who has the luxury of rational thought would ever catch barf, but you just did. In a millisecond and in the absence of mental processing, you decided to cup your hand

and form a vomit-catching basket of fingers in order to collect the partially digested food, bile, and possibly some stomach virus rather than having to clean it up. This is parenthood. You have arrived.

THE "I NO LONGER GIVE A FUCK WHAT I LOOK LIKE AND WEAR PAJAMAS IN PUBLIC" BADGE. I'm not talking about the black yoga pants so many of us use to conceal the fact that we are sleeping in the same clothes we're wearing to run errands. I'm talking about the mothers and fathers who finally said "FUCK IT" and walked out of the house in striped pj's. Nobody forgets the day it happens to them; the day they stopped caring. Your hair looks like you just crawled out of a sewage pipe, your face is blotchy, and your pajamas are wrinkled and stained, but you're so tired, so beaten down by this thing called toddlerhood, that you grab your keys and let your freak flag fly. We salute you, soldier.

THE "IS THIS CHOCOLATE OR IS THIS POO? TASTE TEST" BADGE. You, my friend, are a gambler. Whether you won and the smudge on the wall or on your child's face was legitimate chocolate, or you lost and got a taste of feces, you have our respect. Yes, you could have done a sniff test, but you live life on the edge and I get it. Maybe you have pinkeye now, maybe you don't, but what you do have for sure is a sense of adventure that we all strive for. Namaste, motherfucker. Namaste.

In Closing

Parents have it hard these days. We might have more gadgets for raising kids, but we're far more neurotic than the generations of moms and dads before us. Nowadays, we're all expected to make lunches in the shape of *Frozen* characters, put our kids in stylish clothes, spend our weekends making elaborate Pinterest-inspired balloon-animal melted-crayon ombre-cookie crafts, and have our families and homes look like they just walked out of a page from *Real Simple* magazine—the pressure is enormous. And it's stupid. No one is keeping score. Raising kids is hard and raising toddlers feels IMPOSSIBLE most of the time. We all wonder if we're fucking it up, so why not just be honest? The kind of people parents need in their lives are the ones they can call to come over for a drink and to bitch about their day while their kids play on the floor. You should be able to say, "Hey, toddlers are assholes," without them getting their panties in a wad. You should be able to say, "I hate my fucking family sometimes" and "Cooking dinner sucks ass." Fuck all this perfectionist, gratitude-out-the-ass bullshit. It's okay to say it sucks when it sucks. Yes, there are people in the world who have it so much worse, but does that mean we can't let off some steam? Of course not.

You know what's hard? Even harder than dealing with toddlers? Pretending it's *not* hard.